500

slow-cooker dishes

500
slow-cooker dishes

the only compendium of slow-cooker dishes you'll ever need

Carol Beckerman

SELLERS
PUBLISHING

A Quintet Book

Published by Sellers Publishing, Inc.
161 John Roberts Road, South Portland, Maine 04106
For ordering information:
(800) 625-3386 Toll Free
(207) 772-6814 Fax
Visit our Web site: www.sellerspublishing.com
E-mail: rsp@rsvp.com

ISBN: 978-1-4162-0662-0
e-ISBN: 978-1-4162-0855-6
Library of Congress Control Number: 2012931293
QTT.FSCM

This book was conceived, designed, and produced by
Quintet Publishing Limited
6 Blundell Street
London N7 9BH
United Kingdom

Food Stylist: Maud Eden
Photographer: Ria Osborne
Art Director: Michael Charles
Editorial Assistant: Holly Willsher
Editorial Director: Donna Gregory
Publisher: Mark Searle

10 9 8 7 6 5 4 3 2 1

Printed in China by 1010 Printing International Ltd.

contents

introduction

Your slow cooker is your best friend. It sits patiently in your kitchen, looking after your dinner, cooking it gently, until you are ready to eat. If you are pushed for time, just a few minutes in the morning is all you need to throw everything in the pot, add some seasoning, and you will arrive home that evening, tired and hungry, to a wonderful aroma as you open the front door.

Even if you work from home or are a stay-at-home mom or dad, the slow cooker will prove itself invaluable. The time before dinner is often stressful. The meal needs attention, the children need attention, homework needs attention, and you are busy, tired, and distracted. How wonderful to have most of the stress removed by the meal being already prepared. When you sit down to eat, it almost feels like someone else has cooked the meal. If your mornings are a mad scramble, with a little planning, you can organize your ingredients the night before. Chop up vegetables, soak beans, marinade meat, and in the morning, boil the beans for a few minutes, then toss it all in the pot. Job done.

There is a fascinating alchemy that happens to the ingredients in a slow cooker as they simmer gently all day, the flavors blending together over the slow cooker's low heat. With the addition of good-quality stock and different herbs and spices, during the long cooking time the flavors develop and deepen, and the simplest of ingredients become rich and satisfying comfort food. With all the natural juices from the meat and vegetables retained in the pot, the dish will be nutritious, tender, and healthy.

A slow-cooked dish is the ultimate in convenience food, with none of the additives found in fast-food meals. You can control the amount of salt and fat. You also save money, because the low cooking temperature means less expensive cuts of meat become tender and shrink less.

The slow cooker needs little or no attention. The heat is so low, the food does not need stirring to keep it from burning. A countertop electrical appliance, a slow cooker cooks foods slowly at a low temperature, usually between 170° and 280°F. The energy used is the same as that of a 75-watt lightbulb, and during hot weather, has the benefit of not adding heat to the kitchen, as an oven or stove does.

Slow cookers are also extremely safe. The direct heat from the pot, the lengthy cooking time, and the steam created within the tightly covered container combine to destroy bacteria, making the slow cooker a safe process for cooking foods.

This book will enable you to discover the versatility of your slow cooker. From soups and stews to cakes and desserts, the recipes will fuel your imagination and inspire you to rely on your slow cooker more than ever before, saving you time and money, and providing you and your family with tasty, new, and interesting meals.

slow cookers & other cooking equipment

Slow cookers are available in a range of sizes and prices. For best results, the slow cooker should be used at least half full, and not more than three-quarters full, so choose an appropriate size for your needs. All the recipes in this book have been tested and prepared in a standard 4-quart slow cooker. The controls on slow cookers vary from one make to another, but all have a low setting and a high setting. As a general rule, food cooked on a low setting takes double the time of that cooked on a high setting, but check your manufacturer's instructions. Some slow cookers also have an automatic setting and a warm or hold setting. The automatic setting starts the slow cooker on a high heat, then, after the temperature has reached the optimum level, it automatically switches to the low setting. The warm or hold setting will keep the temperature of the food at a certain level without any more cooking, which is ideal if you are not quite ready to sit down to eat.

If your slow cooker does not have a rack supplied with it, you could use crumpled aluminum foil to raise dishes off the bottom of the pot when you are steaming or cooking in a water bath. You will need oven gloves for lifting the pot out of the slow cooker and a heatproof mat for protecting your worktop from the hot pot. A heavy-based skillet is essential for browning meat and vegetables before they go into the pot, as well as a large serving spoon or two for transferring food to the slow cooker. You will also need a large saucepan for cooking dried beans and dried peas before they go into the slow cooker, and a colander for draining. A blender, immersion blender, or potato masher will be useful for blending soups and mashing ingredients. If you store food overnight in the refrigerator, freezer bags with a zipper are ideal; then you can just tip them straight into the slow cooker, with no washing up needed in the morning.

slow-cooking techniques

It's not difficult to learn to use a slow cooker, but the following suggestions will be very helpful.

safety tips

Make sure everything is clean before you start. A clean work area, clean utensils, and a clean cooker will keep germs to a minimum. Wash your hands, before, during, and after food preparation and especially after touching raw meat. Keep perishable foods in the refrigerator until you need them. If you prepare the meat and vegetables the night before, store them separately in the refrigerator overnight. Always thaw frozen meat or poultry before using them in a slow cooker. The outside of the slow cooker can get hot during use, so keep it away from the edge of the work surface, and small children. Do not use the slow cooker to reheat food. Always read the maker's instructions for the safety of your appliance and for user instructions.

browning food before slow-cooking

It is not essential to brown all food before it goes into the slow cooker, but it can help the taste if you do so. No one can doubt that food fried in butter has more taste than food cooked in lard or oil, but for health reasons, fat that is liquid when cold is much better for us than hard fat. Consequently, vegetable oils like olive oil and canola oil, are preferred.

If you decide you would like to brown the food first, it will definitely enhance the flavor, and if you have the time, it is worth the effort for the end result. One of the benefits of

browning the food is that after frying the meat and vegetables, you can add the stock or wine to the pan and deglaze, scraping up all the wonderful crispy bits in the bottom of the pan, which are full of flavor. One disadvantage of browning the food first is that it adds a little fat to the dish, problematic if you are following a low-fat diet.

stocks & liquids

During the time the food is cooking, you will find that there is little evaporation from your slow cooker. Consequently, the amount of liquid that you add during preparation is quite important. While the vegetables are cooking, they will give off their own liquid, which adds to the amount in the pot. You do not want too much liquid because it will dilute the flavor of the dish. So, when converting your favorite recipes to use in your slow cooker, a general rule would be to halve the amount of liquid in the original recipe. If making a stew or soup, for example, you only need enough liquid to barely cover the ingredients.

The liquid you do use when making slow-cooked soups, stews, and casseroles should be a good-quality stock. Good stock makes soup and stews that are much richer in taste, with a more enjoyable and satisfying depth of flavor. There's a recipe in the last chapter to make your own stock, so you can control the amount of salt and fat you use.

seasonings

It is very easy for all food cooked in the slow cooker to end up tasting very similar. If you choose different herbs and spices, you can vary the end result enormously. Adding seasoning at the beginning of cooking makes it easy to add too much salt, and we all need to reduce the amount in our diets. So I recommend you taste your dish before serving it, and add the salt and pepper (I prefer freshly ground black pepper) to taste at this point. This means you get the balance of seasonings right, and you keep your food as healthy as possible.

dairy products

Dairy products such as cream, yogurt, and cheese break down during long cooking periods, so they should not be added until the last hour of cooking. Using full-fat dairy products reduces the likelihood of curdling. Some recipes call for the slow cooker pot to be greased or buttered before use; this is generally for desserts, bread puddings, cakes, and bread, and will help stop the food from sticking to the pot during cooking.

beans, lentils & grains

When using beans or peas, canned or frozen are great if you are pushed for time. If you prefer to use dried beans or peas, pick through them carefully and discard any foreign objects or shrivelled beans, then rinse. Soak them overnight, and then place them in a saucepan, cover with water, and bring to a boil. Turn the heat down and simmer for 10–15 minutes. This shortens the cooking time in the slow cooker and makes the bean or pea cook more evenly.

Lentils do not need any soaking. They can be placed straight into the slow cooker. Most grains do not need soaking or precooking, so they can be placed straight into the slow cooker pot. When using rice, allow 1/4 pint water for each 3 1/2 ounces of rice.

Pasta will overcook very quickly and will become soggy if added at the beginning of a recipe, unless the cooking time is very short. You can, however, add small pasta shapes 30–40 minutes before the end of cooking time, if you wish.

vegetables

When cutting up vegetables for soups, stews, and casseroles, try to cut the vegetables to a similar size. Not only will the dish look better, but also the vegetables will cook more evenly. For pot roasts and casseroles, put root vegetables in the bottom of the slow cooker and the meat on top.

Some recipes call for tomatoes that have been skinned, with their seeds removed. To remove the skins, carefully cut around the circumference of the tomato with a sharp knife, place in a bowl, and pour on boiling water. Leave for a minute or two, drain, and the skins should just slide and peel away. Cut the tomatoes in half and scoop out the seeds by running your finger around the inside of the tomato. The seeds will fall out easily.

meat, poultry & seafood

The best cuts of meat to use in the slow cooker are often the cheapest, as the long cooking time is ideal for tenderizing tougher cuts of beef and lamb. When cooking chicken, you will find that boned chicken thighs are a good choice. Chicken breasts, although larger and more convenient, will be slightly drier in texture. Before cooking, trim as much excess fat as possible from meat, and remove the skin from chicken, turkey, and game birds. This will cut down the amount of fat in the dish.

Fish will be the most challenging of all ingredients in your slow cooker. The delicate flesh of white fish such as cod or tilapia will easily fall apart, so it is best cooked for a much shorter time. The firmer fish, such as monkfish, swordfish, and tuna, which have a meaty texture, will be more successful. It is still delicate, however, so at the end of the cooking time, avoid stirring if you can. A good way to cook fish in the slow cooker is to place all the vegetables in the pot and to lay the fish on top, so it is, in effect, steamed, rather than stewed. This helps preserve the integrity of the fish. Do not add shellfish until the last 30–40 minutes of cooking time; cooking it any longer will make it tough.

covering pot

Unless adding extra ingredients, avoid lifting the lid of the slow cooker during cooking time, as each removal increases the cooking time by about 20 minutes. However, the slow cooker is very forgiving if you are delayed in serving your dish. You will find that the heat is so low that food seldom dries out or spoils if the cooking time is extended for an hour—even longer.

sterilizing canning jars

A good way to sterilize jars for preserving is to wash them, place them in the dishwasher, and run them through the hottest cycle. If you do not have a dishwasher, put the jars in a large saucepan, cover with water, and boil the water for 5 minutes. Drain carefully and let cool before using. Either tie on waxed paper and a cloth as a top, or use a screwtop.

soups &
appetizers

Soups are ideal for the slow cooker. The long,

slow cooking time brings out the flavors.

Appetizers such as terrines and pâtés can be

steamed on a rack or trivet, and even bread can

be cooked in the slow cooker.

corn chowder

see variations page 41

This is a very thick and nourishing soup made with frozen corn kernels. The addition of bacon and potatoes makes it a meal in itself and ideal on a cold winter day for lunch.

1 lb. frozen corn kernels
3 3/4 cups water
4 strips bacon, cut into 1/4-inch cubes
2 medium onions, sliced thinly
3 medium-sized potatoes, diced

1 cup half-and-half
1 1/2 cups whole milk
salt and freshly ground black pepper
1/4 cup freshly chopped parsley

Place half the corn with 1 1/4 cups of water in a blender or a food processor and blend until smooth.

In a medium skillet, dry-fry the bacon bits until they are crisp and brown. Remove with a slotted spoon and set aside to drain on a paper towel. Add the sliced onions to the bacon fat in the pan and cook, stirring, until they soften, about 5–6 minutes. Transfer to the slow cooker, stir in the corn puree, the rest of the corn kernels, the potatoes, and the remaining 2 1/2 cups water. Cook on low for 4–5 hours. Half an hour before the end of the cooking time, add the half-and-half and the milk.

To serve, stir in the bacon, check the seasoning, and garnish with the chopped parsley.

Makes 4–6 servings

spicy squash soup

see variations page 42

This soup reminds me of fall, with its rich golden colored leaves. It is low in fat and deliciously spicy and warming as the days get colder.

1 large butternut squash, peeled, halved, and
    seeds removed
1 large carrot, peeled and chopped
2 tbsp. vegetable oil
1 large onion, thinly sliced
1 clove garlic, crushed
1 tsp. peeled and finely chopped gingerroot

1/2 tsp. ground cumin
1/2 tsp. ground coriander
1/2 tsp. garam masala
4 cups vegetable stock
salt and freshly ground black pepper
freshly chopped chives, to serve
crème fraîche, to serve

Cut the squash into large cubes, and place in the slow cooker with the carrot. Heat the vegetable oil in a large saucepan, add the onion, garlic, ginger, and spices. Stir well. Cover and cook for about 10 minutes, over medium heat, stirring occasionally and checking that the spices do not burn. Add the stock and bring to a boil for a few minutes.

Transfer to the slow cooker, and season to taste. Cook on low for 6–8 hours, or on high for 3–4 hours. If you like a smooth-textured soup, puree in a blender or in the slow cooker with an immersion blender.

To serve, taste for seasoning and adjust if necessary. Serve with a little crème fraîche and sprinkle with freshly chopped chives.

Makes 6 servings

chicken broth

see variations page 43

To make this soup, first you need to cook a chicken and eat most of the meat. You then simmer the carcass for 8–10 hours in the slow cooker so all the goodness from the bones can make a really lip-smacking soup.

1 cooked chicken carcass
1 large onion, finely chopped
2 carrots, peeled and chopped
2 stalks celery, sliced
1 bay leaf
2 vegetable stock cubes
about 5 cups water

to finish the broth
2 carrots, peeled and finely chopped
2 leeks, washed and finely chopped
2 stalks celery, finely chopped
freshly chopped parsley, to serve

With a small sharp knife, remove all the last bits of chicken that remain on the carcass. Put them in a small bowl, cover, and refrigerate. Put the chicken carcass and the chopped vegetables in the slow cooker. Add the stock cubes and enough water to cover the chicken. Do not fill the slow cooker more than two thirds full. Cook on low for 8–10 hours.

Remove the chicken carcass from the slow cooker, and discard. Strain the stock into a large bowl. Wash the slow cooker, and put the stock back in. Add the extra vegetables to finish the broth and cook on high for 1–2 hours. Ten minutes before the end of the cooking time, add the leftover bits of chicken and salt and freshly ground black pepper to taste. Serve sprinkled with some chopped parsley.

Makes 6 servings

leek & potato soup

see variations page 44

This soup is one of the easiest and tastiest soups of all. Rich, satisfying, and full of flavor, it has been a staple in kitchens for a long time.

4 large potatoes, peeled and diced
3 large leeks, washed and sliced
1 large onion, finely chopped
2 vegetable stock cubes

4 cups chicken or vegetable stock
4 tsp. chopped fresh tarragon
salt and freshly ground black pepper
freshly chopped parsley, to serve

Put the potatoes, leeks, onion, and vegetable stock cubes in the slow cooker. Add the stock, and cook on low for 8 hours. Just before serving, add the tarragon, and season to taste. Serve sprinkled with some chopped parsley, if using.

Makes 6 servings

french onion soup

see variations page 45

The secret to delicious French onion soup is using a base of really good beef stock, and cooking the onions slowly until they are caramelized—giving the soup its dark color.

5 large onions, thinly sliced
4 tbsp. butter
6 cups good-quality beef stock
freshly ground black pepper

to serve (optional but traditional)
1/2 cup shredded cheddar cheese
1/4 cup shredded Parmesan cheese
6 slices crusty French bread

Grease the slow cooker, add the onions and butter, and stir together. Cook on high for 10-12 hours, checking occasionally to make sure the edges are not burning, or too dry, and give a stir if necessary. After this time the onions will have caramelized beautifully, so add the beef stock and pepper to taste. Cover and cook on high for 1 hour.

To serve, mix the cheeses together and sprinkle a little on each slice of bread. Put a slice into the bottom of each soup bowl, then ladle the soup on top. Serve immediately.

Makes 6 servings

mulligatawny soup

see variations page 46

Meaning literally "pepper water," mulligatawny is spicy, satisfying, unusual, and interesting.

1 tbsp. butter
1 lb. piece of lean boneless lamb
2 onions, finely chopped
1 carrot, finely chopped
1 small apple, peeled, cored, and chopped
2 tsp. curry powder

2 tsp. mild curry paste
1 tbsp. flour
6 cups water or vegetable stock
salt and freshly ground black pepper
2/3 cup whole milk
2 tbsp. freshly chopped parsley, to serve

Melt the butter in a medium skillet and brown the meat lightly on all sides. Remove the meat and set aside. Add the onions, carrot, and apple to the skillet, and cook for 3–4 minutes. Add the curry powder and curry paste, and cook gently for 3 minutes. Add the flour to the skillet, stirring to combine with the other ingredients, and gradually add 2 cups of water or vegetable stock. Bring to a boil, stirring continuously, then transfer to the slow cooker, and add the rest of the water or stock. Add the meat, season with salt and freshly ground black pepper, cover, and cook on low for 8 hours. Half an hour before the end of the cooking time, add the milk.

Turn off the slow cooker, lift out the meat carefully with a slotted spoon, and set aside. Blend the soup in batches in a blender or blend in the slow cooker with an immersion blender. If you use the blender, you can blend in about a quarter of the meat. Blend the soup until it has the texture you like. Taste and adjust the seasoning as needed. To serve, chop a little of the remaining meat and sprinkle some on each portion along with some freshly chopped parsley.

Makes 6 servings

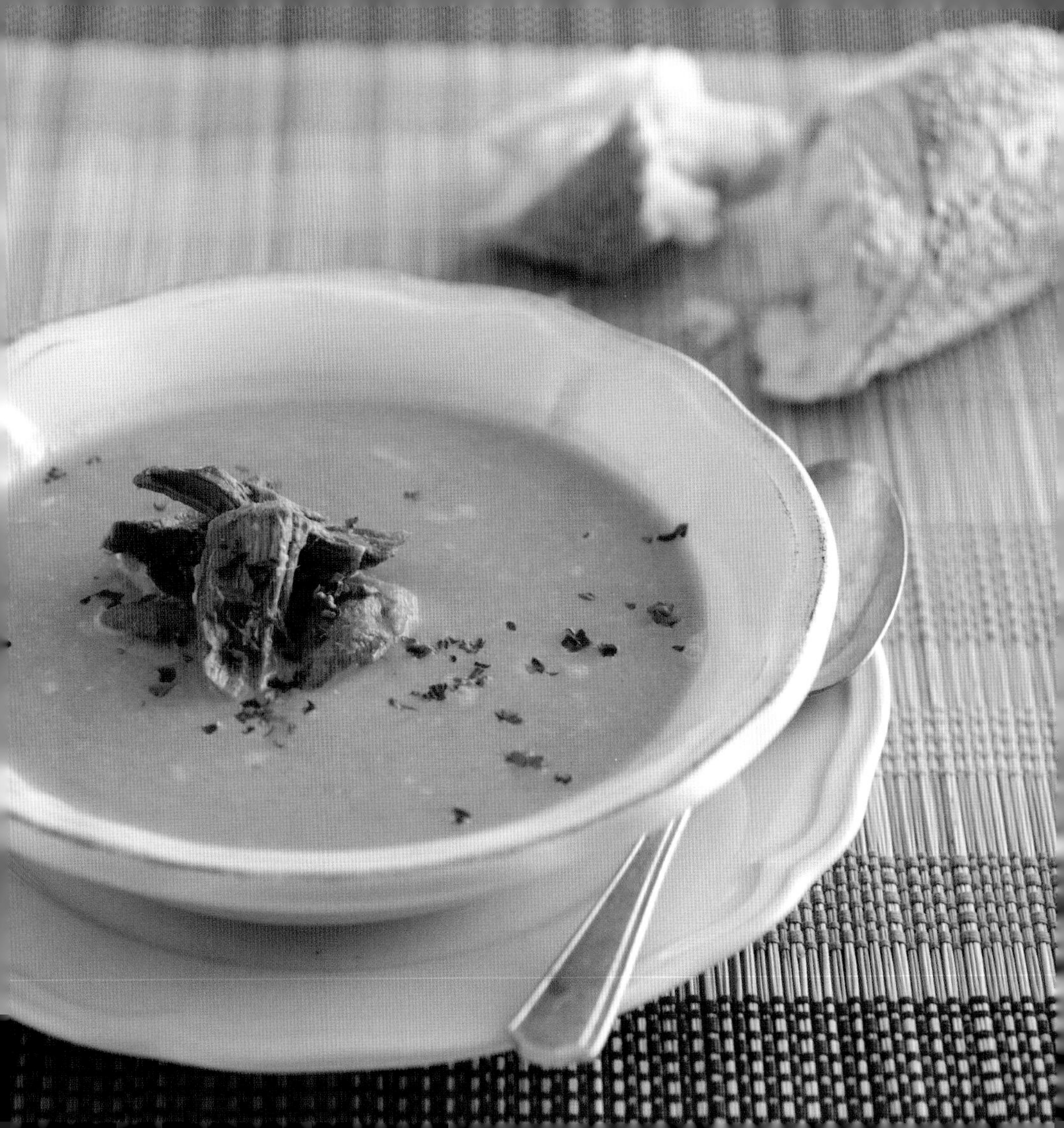

pea & ham soup

see variations page 47

Whether you purchase a ham hock from the butcher or use a meaty bone left over from your baked ham dinner, this is a delicious soup! An added bonus—it freezes well.

1 lb. split green or yellow peas, rinsed and
    picked over
1 meaty ham hock
2 carrots, peeled and diced
1 large potato, peeled and diced

1 large onion, finely chopped
2 stalks celery, sliced
1 bay leaf
5 cups water
salt and freshly ground black pepper

Place the split peas in the slow cooker, place the ham hock on top, and then add the carrots, potato, onion, celery, and bay leaf. Add the water, and do not stir. Cover and cook on low for 8 hours or on high for 4–6 hours. The meat should fall off the bone easily. Remove the ham, and discard the bone, fat, and skin. Chop the meat and return it to the soup. If you like the soup a little thicker, blend it slightly with an immersion blender or mash the peas a little. Taste and adjust the seasoning if necessary. Sprinkle with some chopped parsley just before serving.

Makes 6–7 servings

rustic vegetable soup

see variations page 48

This is a hearty, thick, and filling soup, excellent to come home to on a cold Sunday afternoon after a brisk and invigorating walk. Try to cut the vegetables into similar-sized pieces; the soup looks better that way. Split peas do not need soaking before being cooked in a slow cooker.

2 tbsp. butter (or 2 tbsp. vegetable oil)
2 large onions, coarsely chopped
2 leeks, washed and sliced
1 rutabaga, peeled and diced
1 white turnip, peeled and diced
2 stalks celery, sliced

1 cup split green or yellow peas, washed and
   drained
1 (14-oz.) can chopped tomatoes
4 cups vegetable stock
salt and freshly ground black pepper

In a large saucepan, melt the butter over medium heat. Add the onions and cook gently for 5 minutes, or until softened but not colored. Add the leeks and continue cooking for 2 minutes. Add the rutabaga, turnip, and celery. Cook gently for 5 minutes, stirring frequently. Stir in the split peas, the chopped tomatoes, and the vegetable stock, and bring to a boil. Transfer to the slow cooker and cook on low for 6–8 hours, until the vegetables are tender and soft. Add the salt and freshly ground black pepper to taste.

Makes 8 servings

farmhouse pâté

see variations page 49

This coarse-textured pâté makes a substantial appetizer with toast, or a delicious supper with French bread and a glass of red wine. You will need a medium-sized loaf pan that will fit in your slow cooker, or use a baking dish if necessary.

1 lb. ground veal or pork
8 oz. pork liver, minced
4 oz. pork fat, minced
1 shallot, very finely chopped
1 clove garlic, crushed
2/3 cup port wine

3 slices white bread, crusts removed
2 large eggs, beaten
1/4 tsp. ground allspice
1 tsp. chopped fresh thyme
pinch salt
6–8 strips bacon

Put the ground veal or pork, pork liver and fat, shallot, and garlic into a medium-sized bowl. Put the bread into another bowl, pour in the port wine, and leave until well soaked. Add the soaked bread to the meats with the beaten eggs, allspice, thyme, and salt. Beat thoroughly or put into a blender and blend until smooth. Line the loaf pan with the strips of bacon, and fill with the pâté mixture, pressing into the corners with the back of a spoon. Smooth the top and cover with buttered foil or a double sheet of waxed paper, tied on.

Put a saucer in the bottom of the slow cooker, and place the loaf pan on top. Fill the slow cooker with water until it is halfway up the sides of the loaf pan. Cook on high for 3–4 hours or on low for 6–8 hours. Remove the loaf pan from the slow cooker. Press down the pâté in the pan with a light weight (about 2 pounds) and leave until completely cooled. Chill in the refrigerator. To serve, turn out and cut into slices.

Makes 6 servings

duck & orange pâté

see variations page 50

Slow cookers are ideal for cooking pâtés, which need a long, slow cooking time in a water bath. Serve slices of pâté on salad greens with melba toast and cranberry sauce.

1 duck
1 duck liver
8 oz. ground veal
2/3 cup breadcrumbs
1 medium onion, finely chopped
1 tbsp. freshly chopped thyme leaves

3 tbsp. freshly chopped parsley
salt and freshly ground black pepper
grated rind of 1 orange
2 tbsp. brandy
2 eggs, lightly beaten
4 strips bacon

Butter a 1-pound terrine dish that will fit into your slow cooker. Either ask your butcher to skin and bone the duck, or cut the meat from the duck yourself. The bones can be used for stock. Grind the duck meat coarsely with the duck liver.

In a large bowl, mix the duck meat with the ground veal, breadcrumbs, onion, herbs, salt, and pepper. Stir in the orange rind, brandy, and eggs. Spoon the pâté into the buttered terrine dish and cover with strips of bacon. Cover with foil or tie on a double sheet of waxed paper.

Place a rack or a saucer in the bottom of the slow cooker and place the terrine on top. Add enough water to come halfway up the sides of the terrine, and cook on low for 8 hours or on high for 4 hours. Remove from the slow cooker, let cool, and then refrigerate until needed.

Makes about 8 servings

hummus

see variations page 51

Hummus is a popular and healthy appetizer, spread liberally on griddled pita bread, and served with crudités.

1 1/2 cups dried chickpeas	1/2 cup lemon juice
2 tbsp. extra-virgin olive oil	3/4 cup tahini
1 large onion, finely chopped	2 tbsp. soy sauce
4 cloves garlic, minced	1 tsp. ground cumin
1 carrot, peeled and finely chopped	1/2 tsp. cayenne pepper, or to taste
grated rind of 1 lemon	salt and freshly ground black pepper

In a large saucepan, put the chickpeas and enough water to cover them by 3 inches. Bring to a boil and simmer for 10 minutes. Transfer the chickpeas and the water to the slow cooker. Cook on high for 8–10 hours, or until the chickpeas are soft all the way through and easy to mash. Drain the liquid from the chickpeas into a bowl and reserve. Place the chickpeas in another bowl, and let cool. Heat the olive oil in a medium skillet, and add the onion, garlic, and carrot. Cook over medium heat until the vegetables are soft and nicely browned.

When the chickpeas are cooled, puree in a blender until smooth, using some of the cooking liquid to get the consistency you like. You may have to do this in several batches. Add the lemon rind, lemon juice, tahini, soy sauce, ground cumin, cayenne pepper, salt and black pepper, and mix well until everything is well blended. Taste the hummus and add a little more seasoning if necessary. If the mixture is still too thick, add a little more cooking liquid. Put the hummus into a serving bowl, cover, and refrigerate.

Makes about 1 1/2 quarts

meatballs with redcurrant sauce

see variations page 52

This takes a little more preparation than most slow cooker recipes, but frying the meatballs before adding them to the slow cooker, the result is worth the extra time.

1 lb. ground beef
1/3 cup breadcrumbs
1/4 cup dried cranberries
1 small onion, very finely chopped
1/2 tsp. salt
1 tsp. freshly ground black pepper
1/2 tsp. ground allspice
1 egg, lightly beaten
2 tbsp. vegetable oil

4–5 tbsp. flour
for the sauce
1 lb. fresh or frozen redcurrants
2 cups light brown sugar
grated rind of 1/2 orange
1 shallot, finely chopped
1/3 cup port wine
1/2 tsp. dried rosemary
freshly chopped parsley, to serve (optional)

In a large bowl, mix the ground beef with the breadcrumbs, cranberries, onion, salt, pepper, allspice, and egg. Stir together until well combined. With your hands, roll the mixture into about 24 meatballs, each about 1 inch in size. In a large skillet, warm the oil over medium heat. Roll each meatball in the flour before frying it in the skillet. Cook the meatballs for a few minutes until browned all over, drain on paper towels, then place in the slow cooker. Do not overcrowd the skillet. When you have browned all the meatballs, prepare the sauce. In a medium saucepan, set over medium heat, combine all the ingredients for the sauce. Bring to a boil. Simmer gently for about 5 minutes and transfer to the slow cooker. Gently turn the meatballs around in the sauce, then cook on low for 3–4 hours. When cooking time is finished, spoon the meatballs into a serving dish with the sauce and serve 4 per person, sprinkled with a little freshly chopped parsley.

Makes 6 servings

focaccia

see variations page 53

It is amazing just how versatile your slow cooker can be, and this bread is a great way to get fresh bread with a minimum of fuss.

for the dough
1 1/4 cups warm water
2 tsp. sugar
1 envelope dried yeast
2 cups all-purpose flour
2 tbsp. sugar
2 tbsp. extra-virgin olive oil
1 tsp. salt

1 1/2 cups all-purpose flour
2 tsp. dried rosemary
for the topping
3 cherry tomatoes
1/2 tsp. coarse sea salt
1 tsp. dried rosemary
1 tsp. extra-virgin olive oil

First make the yeast liquid. In a small bowl, add the sugar to the warm water and stir to dissolve. Sprinkle on the yeast and leave about 10 minutes until it becomes frothy. In a large bowl, place the 2 cups of flour with the sugar, salt, and olive oil. Beat to combine. Add the second amount of flour and the dried rosemary, and continue beating until a stiff dough forms. If it feels dry, add a little more water, and if it feels sticky, add a little more flour. Grease the bottom of the slow cooker and place the dough in the bottom, pressing it down lightly. Make 6 indentations in the surface of the dough with your finger, and put half a cherry tomato in each one. Sprinkle with the salt and rosemary and drizzle the olive oil over the top. Lay 5 paper towels between the top of the slow cooker and the lid. Put a toothpick or similar object between the paper towels and the edge of the slow cooker to allow the steam to escape. Cook on high for 2 hours. Do not lift the lid as it cooks. Loosen the sides with a knife and turn out onto a rack to cool.

Makes 1 loaf

variations

corn chowder

see base recipe page 21

corn & crab chowder
Prepare the basic recipe, adding 1–2 cups cooked white crabmeat 10 minutes before the end of the cooking time.

saffron seafood & corn chowder
Prepare the basic recipe, but 30 minutes before the end of the cooking time, add 8 ounces haddock (preferably smoked), cut into 1-inch pieces. Grind about 15 stems saffron with 1 teaspoon boiling water to a paste and add to the chowder with the haddock.

shrimp & corn bisque
Prepare the basic recipe, adding 2 tablespoons white wine, 1 cup roughly chopped cooked shrimp, and 3 peeled and chopped tomatoes 30 minutes before the end of the cooking time.

corn & clam chowder
Prepare the basic recipe. Wash and scrub 6 large or 12 small clams, cook them over high heat with a splash of water, until the shells open. Remove the clams, cut them into 1/2-inch pieces, and add 30 minutes before the end of the cooking time.

variations

spicy squash soup

see base recipe page 22

thai curry & coconut squash soup
Prepare the basic recipe, replacing 2 cups stock with 1 (14-ounce) can coconut milk, and adding 1 tablespoon red Thai curry paste with the spices.

spicy squash & parsnip soup
Prepare the basic recipe, replacing the carrot with 1 or 2 parsnips.

spicy squash soup with cilantro pesto
Prepare the basic recipe. For the pesto, put most of the leaves from 2 bunches of cilantro into a blender with 1 crushed clove of garlic and the grated rind and juice of 1 lemon. Whiz to a paste, then slowly add 1/ 4 cup extra-virgin olive oil. Garnish each serving with 1 teaspoon pesto and a few extra cilantro leaves.

spicy squash & leek soup with saffron cream
Prepare the basic recipe, adding 1 chopped leek with the onion. For the saffron cream, grind about 20 saffron stems with 1 teaspoon boiling water in a mortar, then blend with 1/4 cup crème fraîche. Garnish each serving with a spoonful of saffron cream and a sprinkling of fresh parsley.

variations

chicken broth

see base recipe page 24

chicken noodle soup
Prepare the basic recipe, adding 1/2 pound angel hair pasta 30 minutes before the end of cooking time.

thai coconut chicken soup
Prepare the basic recipe, omitting 1 cup water from the first stage of cooking. Add 1 tablespoon Thai red curry paste and 1 cup coconut milk to the second stage of cooking.

zucchini & chicken soup
Prepare the basic recipe to the second stage. Replace the carrots, leeks, and leftover chicken with 1 1/2 pounds chopped zucchini and 2 tablespoons sherry. When finished cooking, blend until smooth with 1/2 cup heavy cream.

chilled watercress soup
Prepare the basic recipe to the second stage. Omit the carrots, leftover chicken, and parsley. Add 3 bunches of watercress, stalks removed and leaves roughly chopped. Cook with the other vegetables. After cooking, blend until smooth. Chill for several hours, then serve with a swirl of heavy cream and a few watercress leaves.

variations

leek & potato soup

see base recipe page 25

spicy sausage, leek & potato soup
Prepare the basic recipe. Just before the soup is finished, roast 6 ounces chopped chorizo, drizzled with a little olive oil, in a medium to hot oven. Blend the soup until smooth and serve with 1 tablespoon roasted chorizo and juices per portion.

leek & potato soup with stilton
Prepare the basic recipe. Garnish each serving with a generous sprinkling of crumbled stilton cheese.

celery, leek & potato soup
Prepare the base recipe, adding 2 stalks chopped celery with the rest of the vegetables.

variations

french onion soup

see base recipe page 27

french onion soup with mushrooms & bourbon
Prepare the basic recipe, adding 1 cup sliced mushrooms and 2 tablespoons bourbon with the stock.

french onion soup with barley & beans
Prepare the basic recipe, adding 1/2 cup quick-cooking barley and 1 drained (14-ounce) can cannellini beans with the stock.

creamed onion soup with cider
Instead of the basic recipe, gently fry the onions in the butter in a large skillet for 15 minutes before transferring to the slow cooker. Add 4 cups beef stock and 2 cups cider. Cook on low for 6–8 hours. Taste and season, add 1/4 cup heavy cream, and blend until smooth. Omit the bread topping. Garnish with freshly chopped parsley.

french onion soup with madeira & gruyère
Prepare the basic recipe, adding 4 tablespoons Madeira with the stock. Replace the cheddar with Gruyère.

variations

mulligatawny soup

see base recipe page 28

mulligatawny soup with beans & barley
Prepare the basic recipe, adding 1/2 cup dried navy beans and 1/2 cup pearl barley to the soup with the meat.

mulligatawny soup with tomatoes
Prepare the basic recipe, adding 1 (14-ounce) can chopped tomatoes with their juice to the soup with the meat.

mulligatawny soup with root vegetables
Prepare the basic recipe, adding 1 parsnip, an extra carrot, 1 rutabaga, and 1 white turnip, all peeled and finely chopped, to the soup with the meat.

mulligatawny soup with sweet potato
Prepare the basic recipe, adding 1 peeled and diced sweet potato to the soup with the meat.

variations

split pea soup

see base recipe page 30

smoky split pea & black bean soup
Prepare the basic recipe, adding 1 tablespoon smoked paprika and 1 drained
(14-ounce) can black beans to the soup with the vegetables.

split pea & basil soup
Prepare the basic recipe, adding 1 bunch basil, leaves only, with the vegetables.

split pea & fresh pea soup
Prepare the basic recipe. To serve, put 2 tablespoons cooked and drained fresh
peas in each bowl, and add the soup.

split pea & butter bean soup
Prepare the basic recipe, adding 1 drained (14-ounce) can butter beans to the
soup with the vegetables.

variations

rustic vegetable soup

see base recipe page 32

rustic cabbage soup with butter beans
Prepare the basic recipe, replacing the rutabaga with 1 chopped head Savoy cabbage, and 1 (14-ounce) can butter beans, drained, for the split peas.

rustic vegetable soup with croutons & pesto
Prepare the basic recipe. Make croutons by cutting 3 slices stale bread into cubes. Fry in a little extra-virgin olive oil with 1 chopped clove garlic. Sprinkle each serving with croutons and 1 teaspoon prepared pesto.

rustic vegetable soup with lentils
Prepare the basic recipe, replacing the split peas with 1 cup green puy (French) lentils.

rustic minestrone
Prepare the basic recipe, replacing the split peas with 1/2 head Savoy cabbage, chopped, and 1 pound dried cannellini beans, soaked overnight and boiled for 10 minutes. Thirty minutes before the end of the cooking time, add 3/4 pound spaghetti, snapped into pieces.

variations

farmhouse pâté

see base recipe page 33

farmhouse pâté with cranberries
Prepare the basic recipe, adding 1/4 cup dried cranberries to the pâté when you remove it from the blender.

farmhouse pâté with mushrooms & parsley
Prepare the basic recipe, adding 1/4 cup chopped mushrooms and 2 tablespoons freshly chopped parsley to the blender with the pâté.

farmhouse pâté with chestnuts
Prepare the basic recipe, adding 1/4 cup finely chopped cooked chestnuts to the pâté when you remove it from the blender.

farmhouse pâté with apple & walnuts
Prepare the basic recipe, adding 1 peeled and finely chopped apple and 1/4 cup chopped walnuts to the pâté when you remove it from the blender.

farmhouse pâté with pheasant & juniper berries
Prepare the basic recipe, replacing 1/2 pound veal (or pork) with 1/2 pound ground pheasant. Add 2 teaspoons crushed juniper berries to the pâté with the allspice and thyme.

duck & orange pâté

see base recipe page 34

duck & cherry pâté

Prepare the basic recipe, replacing the orange zest with 1/4 cup dried cherries. Serve with cranberry sauce.

hoisin duck pâté with scallions

Prepare the basic recipe, replacing the orange zest, brandy, and thyme leaves with 2 tablespoons hoisin sauce and 2 tablespoons finely chopped scallions.

duck & prune pâté with armagnac

Prepare the basic recipe, replacing the orange zest and brandy with 1/4 cup chopped dried prunes and 2 tablespoons armagnac. Serve with plum chutney. To make the chutney, cut 1 pound red plums in half and discard pits. Heat gently with 3/4 cup sugar, 1/2 cup cider vinegar, 1 cinnamon stick, and 2 star anise until sugar dissolves. Bring to a boil, then simmer gently until the plums are tender and the liquid syrupy, about 25–30 minutes. Discard cinnamon and star anise and chill.

duck pâté with apple & fennel

Prepare the basic recipe, replacing the orange zest with 1 small peeled and finely chopped apple and 1 teaspoon lightly roasted fennel seeds.

variations

hummus

see base recipe page 36

hummus with roasted red bell peppers
Prepare the basic recipe. Add 2/3 cup lightly sautéed and chopped red bell peppers, to the hummus after blending.

hummus with black beans
Prepare the basic recipe. Add 1 drained (14-ounce can) black beans to the hummus with the tahini.

hummus with chipotle peppers & cilantro
Prepare the basic recipe. Add 2 mild canned chipotle peppers and 1/4 cup freshly chopped cilantro to the hummus with the tahini.

hummus with sun-dried tomatoes & basil
Prepare the basic recipe. Add 3 tablespoons chopped sun-dried tomatoes and 1/4 cup freshly chopped basil to the hummus with the tahini.

hummus with roasted garlic & spinach
Prepare the basic recipe. Add 1 bulb garlic, roasted in the oven for 20 minutes and cooled, to the hummus, before blending, and 1/2 cup lightly steamed and chopped fresh spinach after blending.

variations

meatballs with redcurrant sauce

see base recipe page 39

meatballs with barbecue sauce
Prepare the basic recipe, replacing the sauce with barbecue sauce (page 94).

lamb meatballs with redcurrant sauce
Prepare the basic recipe, replacing the ground beef with ground lamb. To serve, sprinkle with freshly chopped mint instead of parsley.

open lasagna with tiny meatballs
Prepare the basic meatballs and omit the cranberry sauce. To serve, for each portion, layer a square of cooked lasagna noodle, 1 tablespoon tomato sauce (page 269), 3 or 4 meatballs, 1 tablespoon shredded cheddar cheese, and repeat. Top with freshly chopped basil.

pork meatballs with satay sauce
Prepare the basic recipe, replacing the ground beef with ground pork and the redcurrant sauce with satay sauce (page 118).

turkey meatballs in cranberry sauce
Prepare the basic recipe, replacing the ground beef with ground turkey and the redcurrant sauce with cranberry sauce (page 264).

variations

focaccia

see base recipe page 40

focaccia with red onion & olives
Prepare the basic recipe, replacing the cherry tomatoes in the topping with
1 red onion, sliced into wedges, and 8 pitted black olives.

focaccia with sun-dried tomatoes & anchovies
Prepare the basic recipe, replacing the cherry tomatoes in the topping with
4 halved sun-dried tomatoes and a few anchovies.

focaccia with roasted red bell peppers & rosemary
Prepare the basic recipe, replacing the cherry tomatoes in the topping with
1/2 red bell pepper, sliced and roasted, and 1 extra teaspoon rosemary.

focaccia with roasted garlic & thyme
Prepare the basic recipe, replacing the tomatoes and rosemary in the topping
with 1 roasted garlic bulb, pulled apart into cloves, and 1 teaspoon thyme.

focaccia with tomatoes & parmesan
Prepare the basic recipe, adding 2 tablespoons freshly grated Parmesan cheese
to the topping.

fish & shellfish

It can be quite difficult to cook fish in a slow cooker. Because of the delicate nature of fish, it can sometimes dry out and fall apart. Several firm-fleshed fish, however, like monkfish and salmon, cook very well in a slow cooker.

chinese salmon

see variations page 68

If you cannot find baby bok choy, use two or three large ones. The bean sprouts are added at the very end because they would disintegrate during cooking. Serve with Chinese rice noodles tossed with a little olive oil.

2 sweet onions, thinly sliced
1 red bell pepper, seeded and sliced
4–6 baby bok choy, washed
2 cups sliced mushrooms
4 oz. baby corn, fresh or canned
4 oz. sugar snap peas
1 tbsp. vegetable oil
2 tsp. Chinese five-spice powder

1 mild green chili, seeded and finely chopped
1 clove garlic, crushed
1 tsp. peeled and finely chopped gingerroot
2/3 cup teriyaki sauce
4 salmon fillets
freshly ground black pepper
1/2 lb. fresh bean sprouts
freshly chopped cilantro, to serve

Place the sliced onions in the bottom of the slow cooker. Add the red bell pepper. Remove the stalk end of the bok choy, and add to the slow cooker with the mushrooms, sugar snap peas, and corn.

In a small saucepan on low heat, heat the vegetable oil. Add the five-spice powder, chili, garlic, and ginger, and cook for 2 minutes. Stir in the teriyaki sauce, then pour mixture into the slow cooker on top of the vegetables. Place the salmon fillets on top, season to taste with black pepper, cover, and cook on low for 4 hours. At the end of the cooking time, taste and adjust the seasoning if necessary, and tip in the bean sprouts. Leave for 5 minutes, then serve over noodles, garnished with freshly chopped cilantro.

Makes 4 servings

jambalaya

see variations page 69

Although traditionally jambalaya is cooked with rice all in one pot, for the slow cooker, it works better to do the meat and the vegetables together, add the shrimp, and then serve it over rice that has been cooked separately.

1 lb. boneless skinless chicken thighs
1 lb. smoked sausage, cut into 2-inch slices
1 large onion, finely chopped
1 large green bell pepper, seeded and sliced
3 stalks celery, sliced
1 (14-oz.) can chopped tomatoes in juice
3 tbsp. tomato paste
3 cloves garlic, crushed
1 tbsp. Cajun seasoning

1 tsp. dried thyme
1 tsp. dried oregano
1 cup good-quality chicken stock
3/4 lb. large shrimp, peeled and deveined
2 tbsp. freshly chopped basil, to serve
1 1/2 cups cooked long-grain rice, to serve

Cut each chicken thigh in half. Heat the vegetable oil in a large skillet and brown the thighs all over. Place into the slow cooker with the sausage, onion, green pepper, celery, chopped tomatoes, tomato paste, garlic, Cajun seasoning, thyme, and oregano. Add the chicken stock. Cover and cook on low for 7 hours. One hour before the end of the cooking time, taste and adjust the seasoning if necessary, and stir in the shrimp. Cover and finish cooking.

To serve, stir in the basil and serve over rice.

Makes 7–8 servings

mediterranean fish stew

see variations page 70

It is possible to cook fish in the slow cooker, but you need to cook it for less time because it is delicate and can dry out. Be careful not to burn the garlic, as this can make it bitter.

2 tbsp. extra-virgin olive oil
3 cloves garlic, crushed
1 small fennel bulb, halved and shredded
1/2 tsp. dried red pepper flakes
1 tsp. paprika
1/2 cup dry white wine
1 (28-oz.) can whole tomatoes in juice
1 cup chicken or fish stock

1 tsp. dried basil
1 tsp. dried oregano
1 lb. firm-fleshed white fish fillets, cut into
    2-inch pieces
1/2 lb. medium shrimp, peeled and deveined
1/4 cup freshly chopped parsley, to serve

In a large skillet, heat the olive oil over low heat. Add the garlic, cook for 2 or 3 minutes, and add the fennel. Sauté for 5 minutes, until the fennel has softened. Transfer to the slow cooker and add the red pepper flakes, paprika, white wine, tomatoes, stock, and herbs. Cook on low for 5 hours.

One hour before the end of the cooking time, taste and adjust the seasoning if necessary, add the fish and shrimp, and finish cooking. Just before serving, stir in the parsley.

Makes 4 servings

family tuna casserole

see variations page 71

Keep mushroom soup, canned tuna, and fish stock in your cupboard, so this can be your standby recipe when you don't know what else to serve.

6 medium potatoes, peeled and sliced
salt and freshly ground black pepper
1 large onion, finely chopped
3 carrots, peeled and diced
4 tomatoes, chopped
1 large green bell pepper, seeded and finely
  chopped

3 (5-oz.) cans chunk tuna in water, drained
1 (14-oz.) can mushroom soup
1 cup fish stock

Butter the bottom of the slow cooker, and place a third of the potatoes in it. Season them generously with salt and freshly ground black pepper. Cover with a third of the onion, a third of the carrots, a third of the tomatoes and green pepper, and 1 can of tuna. Repeat the layers twice more, pour in the soup and fish stock, cover, and cook on low for 7–10 hours, or until the potatoes are cooked and tender.

Makes 4 servings

swordfish with orange & mango salsa

see variations page 72

This spicy fish dish, with the citrus flavors blending with the hot jerk seasoning, is colorful and bright, and delicious served with basmati rice flavored with a little saffron.

4 swordfish steaks (1 steak per person)
1/4 cup extra-virgin olive oil
2 tbsp. jerk seasoning
1/4 cup freshly squeezed lime juice
3 tbsp. freshly squeezed orange juice
1/4 cup tequila
3 tsp. freshly chopped cilantro
salt and freshly ground black pepper

for the orange & mango salsa
2 ripe mangoes, peeled and diced
3 oranges, peeled and diced
1/2 cup sliced green onions
3 tbsp. freshly chopped cilantro
1/2 tsp. ground ginger
1/2 jalapeño pepper, seeded and finely chopped
juice of 1/2 lime, to serve (optional)

In a bowl, mix the olive oil with the jerk seasoning, lime juice, orange juice, tequila, cilantro, and salt and pepper to taste. Transfer to the slow cooker, place the swordfish steaks on top, cover, and cook on low for 2 hours.

To make the salsa, combine all the ingredients in a bowl. Set aside until ready to serve. Serve the swordfish steaks with the salsa and a squeeze of lime, if using.

Makes 4 servings

monkfish with mushrooms & paprika

see variations page 73

Monkfish is an ideal fish for cooking in the slow cooker, but it can lose a lot of milky fluid during cooking. Sprinkle it with salt 30 minutes before using, and let stand, then pat dry with paper towels.

2 medium onions, finely chopped
3 cups sliced mushrooms
2 tbsp. paprika
2 cloves garlic, crushed
salt and freshly ground black pepper

1 cup chicken or fish stock
2 lbs. monkfish tail, cut into 4-inch pieces
2/3 cup sour cream

Place all the ingredients except the monkfish and the sour cream into the slow cooker and give them a good stir to combine. Add the monkfish and turn it around gently to coat with the sauce.

Cover and cook on low for 4 hours. Just before serving, taste and adjust the seasoning if necessary, and stir in the sour cream.

Makes 6 servings

easy gumbo

see variations page 74

The word "gumbo" is derived from the African word, gombo, meaning okra. It is a soup or stew from the New Orleans area, and when made with seafood is generally acknowledged to be a creole dish.

1/2 lb. bacon, chopped
1 medium onion, finely chopped
2 stalks celery, chopped
1 large green bell pepper, seeded and chopped
2 cloves garlic, crushed
2 cups chicken stock
1 (14-oz.) can chopped tomatoes in juice
2 tbsp. Worcestershire sauce
2 tsp. dried thyme
1 tsp. dried oregano

1 tsp. paprika
1 bay leaf
1/2 tsp. cayenne pepper
salt and freshly ground black pepper
1 lb. medium shrimp, peeled and deveined
1 lb. crabmeat, fresh or frozen
1 (10-oz.) package frozen okra, sliced into
    1/2-inch pieces
2 tsp. cornstarch mixed with a little cold water
freshly chopped parsley, to serve (optional)

In a large skillet, over medium heat, cook the bacon until crisp and golden. Remove with a slotted spoon to the slow cooker. Drain off most of the fat from the skillet, and add the onion, celery, green pepper, and garlic. Cook over medium heat for 5 minutes and transfer to the slow cooker. Add the stock, tomatoes, Worcestershire sauce, thyme, oregano, paprika, bay leaf, and cayenne pepper to the slow cooker. Season with salt and pepper. Cover and cook on low for 5 hours. One hour before the end of the cooking time, add the shrimp, crabmeat, and okra. Ten minutes before the end of the cooking time, taste and adjust the seasoning if necessary, and thicken the sauce with a little cornstarch mixed with water. Leave for another 10 minutes, and serve sprinkled with freshly chopped parsley, if using.

Makes 6 servings

goan fish curry

see variations page 75

Use any firm-fleshed white fish and do not add too much tamarind, because it can make the dish bitter.

4 cardamom pods, seeds only
1 tsp. coriander seeds
2 tsp. mustard seeds
2 tbsp. shredded unsweetened coconut
2 tbsp. olive oil
1 large onion, coarsely chopped
4 cloves garlic, crushed
2 tsp. peeled and finely chopped gingerroot
2 mild red chilies
1 tsp. each ground cumin, turmeric, and paprika

1/2 tsp. garam masala
2 tsp. tamarind paste
1 tsp. ground cinnamon
2 1/4 cups coconut milk
1 1/2 lbs. firm-fleshed white fish fillets, cut
    into 4-inch pieces
1 small potato, peeled and diced quite small
12 large shrimp, peeled, and deveined
4 tbsp. freshly chopped cilantro
2 tomatoes, chopped, to serve

In a small saucepan over medium heat, dry-fry the cardomon seeds, coriander seeds, and mustard seeds, until they begin to jump. Remove from heat, tip into a mortar, and grind to a powder with the pestle. Set aside. Add the coconut to the saucepan and toast until golden brown. Remove from heat and set aside. In a medium skillet, heat the oil, and cook the onion for 5 minutes. Add the garlic, ginger, chilies, cumin, turmeric, paprika, garam masala, and cook for 2 minutes. Tip in the ground spices, toasted coconut, and tamarind paste. Transfer to the slow cooker, and add the coconut milk. Stir together to combine. Place the fish and potato in the sauce, cover, and cook on low for 4 hours. Thirty minutes before the end of cooking time, add the shrimp and stir gently to coat in sauce. Before serving, adjust the seasoning as needed, stir in the cilantro, and garnish with chopped tomato.

Makes 4 servings

variations

chinese salmon

see base recipe page 55

salmon with green thai curry sauce

Prepare the basic recipe, omitting the baby corn, five-spice powder, and bean sprouts. Replace red bell pepper with green pepper and teriyaki sauce with 2/3 cup coconut milk and 2 tablespoons green Thai curry paste.

salmon with korean barbecue sauce

Prepare the basic recipe, omitting the teriyaki sauce. Make Korean barbecue sauce by cooking 2 teaspoons dark sesame oil, 2 crushed cloves garlic, 1 tablespoon soy sauce, 3 tablespoons teriyaki sauce, 1/2 teaspoon salt, and 1/4 cup packed brown sugar, until the sugar has dissolved.

salmon with black bean sauce

Prepare the basic recipe, omitting the teriyaki sauce. Make black bean sauce by heating 1 tablespoon peanut oil in a saucepan, then adding 2 (15-ounce) cans black beans, drained and lightly crushed, 2 cloves garlic, 1 tablespoon soy sauce, 2 tablespoons rice wine, 1 teaspoon sugar, and 2 teaspoons cornstarch mixed with 2/3 cup chicken stock. Bring to a boil and simmer for 2 minutes.

variations

jambalaya

see base recipe page 56

jambalaya with egg & pancetta
Prepare the basic recipe, adding 1/2 cup chopped pancetta with the shrimp.
Ten minutes before the end of the cooking time, add 2 hard-boiled and
chopped eggs.

jambalaya with red kidney beans
Prepare the basic recipe. Add 1 (14-ounce) can red kidney beans, drained, to
the jambalaya with the herbs.

clambalaya
Prepare the basic recipe. Wash and scrub 6 large or 12 small clams, and cook in
a saucepan with a splash of water, over high heat, until the shells open.
Remove the clams from their shells, cut them into 1/2-inch pieces, and add to
the jambalaya just before the end of the cooking time.

crabalaya
Prepare the basic recipe. Add 1 cup crabmeat to the jambalaya with the shrimp.

variations

mediterranean fish stew

see base recipe page 58

mediterranean fish stew with pancetta
Prepare the basic recipe, adding 1/2 cup chopped pancetta to the stew with the fish and shrimp.

mediterranean fish stew with olives & eggplant
Prepare the basic recipe, omitting the shrimp. Cut 1 medium eggplant into cubes and add to the stew with the stock and herbs. Add 1/4 cup pitted black olives to the stew with the fish.

mediterranean fish stew with mussels
Prepare the basic recipe, omitting the shrimp. Add 2 cups of very fresh and clean mussels to the stew with the fish.

mediterranean fish stew with lobster
Prepare the basic recipe, omitting the shrimp. Add 1 cup canned or fresh lobster meat to the stew with the fish.

variations

family tuna casserole

see base recipe page 59

family tuna casserole with jalapeño peppers & swiss cheese
Prepare the basic recipe, adding 2 chopped jalapeño peppers and 1 cup shredded Gruyère cheese to the layers.

family tuna casserole with green onions & corn
Prepare the basic recipe, omitting the carrots. Add 1/2 cup chopped green onion and 1 cup corn kernels to the layers.

family tuna casserole with sweet potatoes & asparagus
Prepare the basic recipe, replacing the potatoes and green bell pepper with sweet potatoes and 8–10 asparagus spears.

variations

swordfish with orange & mango salsa

see base recipe page 60

swordfish with black bean & corn salsa

Prepare the basic recipe, omitting the salsa. Mix 1 drained (14-ounce) can
black beans with 1 drained (14-ounce) can whole kernel corn. Add 2
tablespoons extra-virgin olive oil, and 1/4 cup freshly chopped cilantro.
Serve with the swordfish.

honey & ginger tilapia with black bean & corn salsa

Prepare the basic recipe, omitting the swordfish and substituting tilapia.
Omit the jerk seasoning, lime juice, and tequila. Substitute 2 teaspoons finely
chopped gingerroot, 2 tablespoons honey, and 1/4 cup fish stock. Serve with
black bean and corn salsa (above).

swordfish with avocado & mango salsa

Prepare the basic recipe. Replace the oranges in the salsa with 1 avocado,
peeled, pitted, and chopped.

salmon with onion salsa

Prepare the basic recipe, replacing the swordfish with 4 salmon fillets. Omit
the orange and mango from the salsa and substitute 1/2 cup chopped red
onion and 2 tablespoons extra-virgin olive oil.

monkfish with mushrooms & paprika

see base recipe page 62

monkfish & mushrooms in barbecue sauce
Prepare the basic recipe, omitting the garlic, paprika, stock, and sour cream.
Substitute barbecue sauce (page 94).

monkfish, mushrooms & shrimp with cashews
Prepare the basic recipe, adding 3 ounces peeled and deveined shrimp and
1/4 cup cashews to the slow cooker 30 minutes before serving.

monkfish & mushrooms with kalamata olives & lemon salsa
Prepare the basic recipe, omitting the paprika and sour cream. Make the salsa by
finely chopping 4 stalks celery, 1 cup pitted kalamata olives, 1 green seeded
chili, 1 clove garlic, 2 tablespoons each of freshly chopped parsley and basil. Mix
with 2 tablespoons extra-virgin olive oil and season with salt and freshly ground
black pepper. Serve with the monkfish.

monkfish & parma ham with mushrooms & paprika
Prepare the basic recipe, wrapping each piece of monkfish in 2 slices of parma
ham before cooking.

variations

easy gumbo

see base recipe page 64

easy gumbo with mixed seafood
Prepare the basic recipe. Add 6 shucked oysters to the gumbo with the shrimp and crabmeat.

easy gumbo with sausage
Prepare the basic recipe, adding 1/2 cup spicy sausage cut into 1-inch pieces to the gumbo with the shrimp and crabmeat.

easy gumbo with squid
Prepare the basic recipe, adding 1/2 cup raw squid to the gumbo with the shrimp and crabmeat.

easy gumbo with mussels
Prepare the basic recipe, adding 6 scrubbed mussels to the gumbo with the shrimp and crabmeat.

easy gumbo with basil & olives
Prepare the basic recipe, adding 1/4 cup freshly chopped basil and 1/4 cup pitted olives to the gumbo 10 minutes before the end of cooking time.

variations

goan fish curry

see base recipe page 67

goan monkfish curry with pancetta
Prepare the basic recipe, using monkfish as the white fish, and adding 1/4 cup chopped pancetta to the gumbo with the shrimp.

goan fish curry with lobster
Prepare the basic recipe, replacing 1/2 pound of white fish with 1/2 pound fresh or canned lobster meat.

goan mixed seafood curry
Prepare the basic recipe, replacing 1/2 pound of white fish with 5 scrubbed mussels and 1/2 cup raw squid.

goan fish curry with scallops & red bell pepper
Prepare the basic recipe, replacing 1/2 pound of white fish with 6 scallops, and adding 2 red bell peppers, seeded and thinly sliced, to the gumbo with the onion and spices.

goan salmon curry with cashews
Prepare the basic recipe, using salmon instead of white fish, and adding 1/2 cup cashews to the gumbo 10 minutes before the end of cooking time.

beef, pork & lamb

A slow cooker is excellent for cooking the cheaper cuts of meat. In fact, they are better than more expensive cuts. Adding good-quality stock makes a huge difference to the taste, and adding wine helps to tenderize and flavor the meat.

carbonnade of beef & dumplings

see variations page 99

When browning meat in the skillet, do not move it around too much; let it sit in the pan to form a nice brown crust before turning it over to brown the other side.

2 lbs. lean beef, with visible fat trimmed, cut
    into 1-inch pieces
salt and freshly ground black pepper
2 tbsp. vegetable oil
2 large onions, thinly sliced
2 cloves garlic, crushed
2 tbsp. flour
3/4 cup good-quality beef stock
1 1/2 cups dark brown ale
2 stalks celery, chopped

2 sprigs fresh thyme
2 bay leaves
1 beef stock cube
1 tbsp. whole-grain mustard
1 tbsp. brown sugar
for the dumplings
1 cup all-purpose flour
1/2 cup frozen butter, grated
pinch salt and freshly ground black pepper
1 tbsp. dried mixed Italian herbs

Season the beef well with salt and pepper. Heat the oil in a large skillet, and fry the meat in batches, until it is browned all over. Transfer meat to the slow cooker. Add a little more oil to the skillet if necessary, add the onions and garlic, and cook for 5 minutes until softened. Add the flour and stir well until incorporated. Add the stock and the ale a little at a time, stirring continuously, until the gravy is thickened. Transfer to the slow cooker and add the celery, thyme, and bay leaves. Cover and cook on low for 8–10 hours. Around 25 minutes before the end of the cooking time, taste the stew, adjust the seasoning if necessary, and stir in the mustard and brown sugar. Make the dumplings. In a medium bowl, use a fork to mix the flour with the butter, a little salt and pepper, and the herbs. Add enough cold water to make a fairly soft dough. Form into 6 round balls, using your floured hands. Twenty minutes before the end of the cooking time, add the dumplings by dropping them lightly into the stew.
Makes 6 servings

beef pot roast

see variations page 100

Few foods satisfy as completely as a beef pot roast. The delicious flavor and the ease of cooking all the vegetables and meat in one pot is hard to beat.

3 lbs. boneless beef chuck
2 tbsp. olive oil
salt and freshly ground black pepper
2 large onions, thinly sliced
3 cloves garlic, crushed
3 tbsp. tomato paste
1 1/2 cups white wine

4 carrots, peeled and sliced
2 cups good-quality beef stock
1 beef stock cube
3 tbsp. Worcestershire sauce
3 sprigs fresh thyme
1 (14-oz.) can butter beans, drained

Pat the roast dry with paper towels, rub both sides with olive oil, and season generously with salt and freshly ground black pepper. Place a large heavy-based skillet over high heat and sear the meat until a dark crust forms on one side, 3–5 minutes. Turn and sear the other side. Remove from the pan and set aside. Lower the heat and add the onions and garlic to the skillet. Cook for 5 minutes until softened, add the tomato paste and wine, and bring to a boil. Simmer until the wine has reduced by half, scraping the bottom of the pan to deglaze. Transfer to the slow cooker, add the carrots, and then place the beef on top of the vegetables. Add the beef stock, stock cube, Worcestershire sauce, and thyme. Cover and cook on low for 8–10 hours.

Thirty minutes before the end of the cooking time, taste, adjust the seasoning if necessary, and add the butter beans. Before serving, remove the thyme if you can find it.

Makes 6 servings

beef daube & herbes de provence

see variations page 101

This is a very similar dish to beef bourguignon. The main difference is the use of herbes de provence—a combination of thyme, marjoram, savory, rosemary, sage, and basil. Either mix your own or buy it in the supermarket.

1/4 cup flour
salt and freshly ground black pepper
2 lbs. lean beef, trimmed and cut into
    2-inch pieces
2 tbsp. olive oil
6 strips bacon, chopped
1 large onion, thinly sliced
3 cloves garlic, crushed
2 cups sliced mushrooms

3 carrots, peeled and sliced
3 tbsp. canned tomato sauce
1 tbsp. herbes de provence
grated zest of 1 orange
1 cup good-quality beef stock
1 beef stock cube
1 cup white wine
1/4 cup pitted black kalamata olives
1/4 cup freshly chopped parsley

Put the flour on a plate and add salt and freshly ground black pepper. Roll the beef in the flour until well coated. In a large skillet, heat the oil and fry the beef in batches until it is nicely browned all over, adding more oil if necessary. Transfer to the slow cooker. Fry the bacon until nicely browned and crisp, and add to the beef. Turn the heat down, discard any excess bacon drippings, and fry the onion and garlic for 5 minutes, until softened.

Transfer to the slow cooker, then add the remainder of the seasoned flour, mushrooms, carrots, tomato sauce, herbs, and orange zest. Pour in the stock, stock cube, and wine. Cover and cook on low for 8–10 hours. Fifteen minutes before the end of the cooking time, taste for seasoning and adjust if necessary, and add the olives and chopped parsley.

Makes 6 servings

steak & guinness pudding

see variations page 102

The word "pudding" comes from the French boudin, meaning "small sausage," referring to encased meats used in Medieval European puddings. Any heatproof, 3-pint glass dish that fits in your slow cooker would work for this dish.

1 1/2 lbs. beef stewing steak, such as skirt
2 tbsp. all-purpose flour
salt and freshly ground black pepper
1 small onion, finely chopped
1 beef stock cube
2 cups all-purpose flour
1 tbsp. baking powder
1 cup frozen butter, grated
1/2 tsp. salt

about 2/3 cup very cold water
6 tbsp. Guinness or other dark beer
2 tbsp. vegetable oil
1 large onion, thinly sliced
2 tsp. all-purpose flour
2 tsp. Dijon mustard
2 tsp. Worcestershire sauce
2 1/2 cups beef stock
salt and freshly ground black pepper

Trim away any fat or gristle from the meat and cut into 1/2-inch pieces. Put 2 tablespoons flour, seasoning, onion, and crumbled stock cube in a large bowl, add the beef, and roll it around until well coated in the flour mix. In a large bowl, mix the flour with the butter and salt. Mix in enough cold water to make a fairly soft dough. Roll out 2/3 of the pastry to a circle large enough to line a greased 3-pint baking dish. Roll out the remaining third to a circle the size of the top of the dish. Put the beef mix in the pastry-lined dish, then add enough Guinness to come to within 1 inch of the top of the dish. Moisten the edges of the pastry "lid" and press it firmly on top. Cover with a sheet of waxed paper, then cover with a sheet of aluminum foil, both pleated to allow for expansion. Tie on with string, making a handle to make it easy to lift out of the slow cooker. Place a rack or a saucer upside down in

the slow cooker, place the dish on top, and pour in enough water to come just under halfway up the side of the dish. Cover and cook on low for 6–8 hours. Make the onion gravy. In a small saucepan, heat the oil and add the onions. Fry them for 5 minutes until softened, stir in the flour, and cook for 1 minute. Stir in the remaining ingredients and bring to a boil, stirring continuously. Simmer for 15 minutes, taste, and adjust the seasoning if necessary. When the cooking time is finished, lift out the pudding carefully, using the string handle. Remove the covering and cut into 4 pieces with a sharp knife. Carefully lift out each portion with a serving spoon, and serve with the onion gravy spooned over.

Makes 4 servings

bolognese sauce for pasta

see variations page 103

This is a great way to get children to eat vegetables, as there are lots of mushrooms, tomatoes, and carrots hidden in the sauce.

1 1/2 lbs. lean ground beef
1 large onion, finely chopped
2 cloves garlic, crushed
1 tbsp. flour
4 tbsp. tomato paste
6 tbsp. canned tomato sauce
1 (14-oz.) can chopped tomatoes in juice
1/2 cup beef stock
1/2 cup hearty red wine
1 beef stock cube

salt and freshly ground black pepper
1 tsp. sugar
1 tbsp. soy sauce
2 carrots, peeled and finely chopped
2 cups finely chopped mushrooms
2 tbsp. freshly chopped basil
2 tsp. cornstarch mixed with a little water
   (optional)
shredded Parmesan cheese, to serve

In a large saucepan, dry-fry the ground beef, stirring to break it up, until browned. Remove, drain off fat, then put beef back in the pan. Add the onion and garlic and cook for 5 minutes. Stir in the flour, then add the chopped tomatoes, tomato paste, tomato sauce, stock, and wine. Season with salt and pepper. Cook for a few minutes over a gentle heat, then add the sugar, soy sauce, carrots, mushrooms, and basil. Stir to combine, and transfer to the slow cooker. Cook on low for 6–7 hours, or high for 3–4 hours. Taste and adjust the seasoning if necessary, and thicken with the cornstarch if you prefer a thicker consistency. Serve over pasta of your choice, sprinkled with freshly chopped basil and Parmesan cheese.

Makes 6 servings

moussaka

see variations page 104

If you can fit your slow cooker pot under the broiler, brown the cheese on the top.

3 tbsp. vegetable oil
1 large onion, finely chopped
2 cloves garlic, crushed
1 1/2 lbs. ground lean beef
5 tbsp. tomato paste
salt and freshly ground black pepper
1/2 lb. potatoes, peeled and sliced
1 large eggplant, sliced
1/2 lb. tomatoes, peeled and sliced

for the cheese sauce
1 tbsp. butter
1 tbsp. flour
1 1/2 cups whole milk
1 1/3 cups shredded cheddar cheese
1 tsp. Dijon mustard
salt and white pepper
1 egg yolk
freshly chopped parsley, to serve

Heat 1 tablespoon oil in a large skillet, add the onion and garlic, and cook until softened. Add the ground beef and cook for a few minutes until browned. Remove from the heat and mix in the tomato paste, salt and pepper. Transfer to the slow cooker. Heat the remaining oil in the skillet, add the potatoes, and fry gently until browned. Remove from the skillet and arrange on top of the meat in the slow cooker. Add the eggplant to the skillet, cook for 5-7 minutes, add sliced tomatoes, and cook for 5 minutes more. Pour mixture over the potatoes. To make the cheese sauce, in a medium saucepan, melt the butter, add the flour, and cook for 2-3 minutes. Stirring continuously over low-medium heat, add the milk a little at a time, until it has all been incorporated. Over low heat, stir in 1 cup of the cheese and mustard. When cheese has melted, season with a little salt and white pepper. Stir in the egg yolk. Pour mixture over the moussaka in the slow cooker. Cover and cook on low for 4-5 hours. At the end of the cooking time, sprinkle the remaining cheese over the top and if you can, place under the broiler to melt the cheese. Serve sprinkled with chopped parsley.

Makes 6 servings

rogan josh

see variations page 105

This is an aromatic lamb curry from Kashmir. If you do not like your food too spicy hot, leave out the chili powder. Serve with naan bread and rice.

2 lbs. lean lamb
1/4 cup flour
salt and freshly ground black pepper
2 tbsp. butter or vegetable oil
2 large onions, thinly sliced
3 cloves garlic, crushed
1 tbsp. ground coriander
1 tbsp. ground cumin
1 tsp. turmeric

1 tsp. finely chopped gingerroot
1 tsp. chili powder
1 tsp. garam masala
1/2 cup chicken stock
1 (14-oz.) can chopped tomatoes in juice
1/2 tsp. sugar
2 tbsp. plain yogurt
2 tbsp. freshly chopped cilantro
1/4 cup sliced almonds, to serve

Trim the lamb of any visible fat and cut into 2-inch pieces. Put the flour onto a plate, season with salt and pepper, and roll the lamb in the flour to coat it all over. In a large skillet, heat the butter or oil, and fry the lamb in batches until nicely browned. Transfer with a slotted spoon to a plate and set aside. Add a little more butter to the pan if necessary, add the onion and garlic, and fry for 5 minutes until softened. Add the coriander, cumin, turmeric, ginger, chili powder, and garam masala, and cook for 3 or 4 minutes. Stir in the rest of the flour, then gradually add 1/2 cup chicken stock and mix well. Add the tomatoes and, stirring continuously to deglaze the pan, bring to a boil. Simmer for 3 minutes, and transfer to the slow cooker. Add the sugar and lamb, stir, and cover. Cook on low for 5–6 hours. Just before serving, stir in the yogurt and chopped cilantro, and taste for seasoning, adjusting if necessary. Serve sprinkled with the sliced almonds.
Makes 6 servings

moroccan lamb tagine

see variations page 106

This spicy tomato and lamb dish goes very well with vegetable and herb couscous. To make the couscous, soak couscous in boiling vegetable stock for 5 minutes off the heat, stir in finely diced cooked vegetables and herbs, and season with black pepper and salt.

1/2 cup flour
salt and freshly ground black pepper
2 1/2 lbs. lean lamb, cut into 1-inch pieces
2 tbsp. vegetable oil
2 onions, thinly sliced
3 cloves garlic, crushed
2 tsp. ground coriander
2 tsp. ground ginger
1 tsp. ground cinnamon
1 tsp. ground turmeric

1 sweet potato, peeled and diced
3 carrots, peeled and diced
1/4 cup Madeira
1 1/2 cups canned tomato sauce
1 cup lamb or chicken stock
1 tbsp. currant jelly
1 tbsp. honey
1 cup pitted dates
2 tbsp. freshly chopped mint

Put the flour on a large plate, and season with salt and freshly ground black pepper. Roll the lamb in the flour until it is well coated. In a large skillet, heat the vegetable oil and fry the lamb over medium to high heat, in two batches, until nicely browned. Transfer the lamb with a slotted spoon to a clean plate and set aside. Add the onions and garlic to the skillet and fry over medium heat for 3–4 minutes, until softened. Add the ground coriander, ginger, cinnamon, and turmeric, and cook for 1 minute more. Transfer to the slow cooker and add the sweet potato, carrots, Madeira, tomato sauce, stock, currant jelly, honey, dates, and any remaining flour. Stir well to combine. Cover and cook on low for 6–8 hours. At the end of the cooking time, taste and adjust the seasoning if necessary. Stir in the mint before serving.

Makes 6 servings

lamb shanks with redcurrant jelly & port

see variations page 107

Lamb shanks are one of the tastiest cuts of meat, and the currant jelly brings out their natural sweetness. As lamb shanks are quite dense, cook on high rather than on low.

1/4 cup flour
salt and freshly ground black pepper
4 lamb shanks
2 tbsp. olive oil
1 large onion, finely chopped
2 tbsp. currant jelly
2 tsp. dried rosemary

1 1/2 cups good-quality chicken stock
1/4 cup port wine
1 tbsp. soy sauce
1 chicken stock cube
2 tsp. cornstarch mixed with a little water (optional)
freshly chopped parsley, to serve

Put the flour on a plate and mix in the salt and pepper. Dredge the lamb shanks in the seasoned flour. Heat the oil in a large skillet and brown the lamb all over. Transfer to the slow cooker. Add the onion to the skillet and fry for 5 minutes, until softened. Add to the lamb with the currant jelly and rosemary. Pour in the stock and port and add the soy sauce and stock cube. Cover and cook on high for 6–7 hours, turning the meat once during cooking if possible.

At the end of the cooking time, taste and adjust the seasoning if necessary. If the sauce seems too thin, thicken it with some cornstarch mixed with a little water. Serve sprinkled with chopped parsley.

Makes 4 servings

lancashire hot pot with scalloped potatoes

see variations page 108

This popular dish in England is now also known as Betty's Hot Pot after a character in the well-known British soap called Coronation Street. Betty makes it every day in the local pub called the Rovers Return and did so for nearly fifty years.

1 1/2 lbs. lean lamb
1/4 cup flour
salt and freshly ground black pepper
3 carrots, peeled and sliced
1 small white turnip, peeled and chopped
1 large onion, finely chopped
1 leek, washed and chopped

1 1/4 lbs. potatoes, peeled and thinly sliced
1 1/4 cups good-quality chicken stock
1 tbsp. tomato paste
1 tsp. dried Italian herbs
freshly chopped parsley, to serve (optional)

Trim any fat from the lamb and cut into neat 1-inch pieces. Put the flour onto a large plate and season with salt and pepper. Roll the meat in the flour until it is well coated. Mix the carrots, turnips, onions, and leek together, and layer with the meat in the slow cooker, seasoning to taste. Finish with a thick layer of sliced potatoes, overlapping them. Mix the chicken stock with the tomato paste and Italian herbs, and pour into the slow cooker. Cover and cook on low for 7–8 hours, or for 4–5 hours on high. Serve sprinkled with some freshly chopped parsley, if using.

Makes 6 servings

lamb stew with herb dumplings

see variations page 109

These dumplings are traditionally made with suet (I prefer vegetable suet), which can sometimes be found in the ethnic aisle in the supermarket. But they are equally as good made with butter. During the cooking process, dumplings soak up the flavor from the stew and are a delicious way of mopping up the gravy.

1/4 cup flour
salt and freshly ground black pepper
2 lbs. lean lamb, cut into 1-inch pieces
2 tbsp. vegetable oil
2 large onions, finely chopped
3/4 cup fresh or frozen peas
2 cups good-quality chicken or lamb stock

1 chicken stock cube
3 large carrots, peeled and chopped
2 tsp. dried mixed Italian herbs
6 dumplings (page 77)

Put the flour onto a plate, add the salt and freshly ground black pepper, and roll the lamb in the flour to coat it all over. Heat the vegetable oil in a large skillet and fry the lamb over medium to high heat in two batches until nicely browned. Transfer with a slotted spoon to a clean plate and set aside. Add the onions to the skillet and cook over medium heat for 2 minutes, until softened. Transfer to the slow cooker, and add any remaining flour, the peas, stock, stock cube, lamb, and carrots. Stir to combine. Cover and cook on low for 6–7 hours. Make 6 dumplings. Twenty minutes before the end of the cooking time, taste the stew and adjust the seasoning if necessary. Drop the dumplings lightly onto the stew, spacing them evenly apart. At the end of the cooking time, the dumplings should be light and fluffy and cooked through.

Makes 6 servings

barbecue baby back ribs

see variations page 110

Ribs always benefit from long slow and gentle cooking, so the slow cooker is ideal for this. They are baked first, then cooked in the slow cooker with barbecue sauce.

2 racks baby back pork ribs
Cajun seasoning
salt and freshly ground black pepper
freshly chopped cilantro and fresh salad greens,
    to serve

for the barbecue sauce
1 cup tomato ketchup
2/3 cup packed brown sugar
1/2 cup dry sherry or Chinese wine
2 tbsp. peeled and finely chopped gingerroot
3 cloves garlic, crushed
1 tbsp. Dijon mustard
1/2 cup soy sauce
3 tbsp. Worcestershire sauce

Heat the oven to 350°F, and line a large roasting or baking pan with foil. Spray with nonstick oil. Season the ribs with plenty of Cajun seasoning, and salt and freshly ground black pepper, place in the pan, and bake for 1 hour. Turn them over after 30 minutes.

In a large bowl, combine all the sauce ingredients and set aside. Remove the ribs from the oven, cut them into portion sizes, and transfer them to the slow cooker. Pour the sauce over the ribs, cover, and cook on low for 8–10 hours. To serve, sprinkle with freshly chopped cilantro and some fresh salad greens.

Makes 4 servings

osso bucco

see variations page 111

This is a dish from Italy of veal marrow bones braised in tomato and wine, and garnished with a colorful Milanese gremolata, which is lemon and parsley mixed together. Ask the butcher to saw the veal into pieces, about 1 1/2 inches long. Serve with buttered noodles for a refreshing summer meal.

3 1/2 lbs. veal shin, washed, dried & any chips
   of bone picked removed
1/4 cup flour
salt and freshly ground black pepper
3 tbsp. butter
1 large onion, finely chopped
2 cloves garlic, crushed
3 carrots, peeled and chopped
2 stalks celery, washed and chopped

1/2 cup white wine
1/2 cup good-quality chicken stock
1 (14-oz.) can chopped tomatoes in juice
1/2 tsp. sugar, or to taste
2 tsp. dried rosemary
for gremolata garnish
4 tbsp. finely chopped parsley
finely grated rind of 2 lemons
2–3 cloves garlic, finely chopped

Dredge the meat with flour seasoned with salt and freshly ground black pepper. In a large skillet, melt the butter 1 tablespoon at a time, and brown the veal pieces in batches. Transfer pieces to the slow cooker, standing them upright in the bottom of the pot. Add a little more butter to the skillet if necessary, and brown the onion, garlic, carrots, and celery. Add to the veal in the slow cooker, then add the wine, stock, tomatoes, sugar, and rosemary. Cover and cook for 7–8 hours on low or for 3–4 hours on high. Shortly before the end of the cooking time, mix together the ingredients for the gremolata. Taste the stew and adjust the seasoning if necessary. Serve sprinkled with gremolata, and with the meat either with the marrow left inside, or extracted and spread on toast.

Makes 6 servings

pork with marsala & prunes

see variations page 112

Marsala wine is very similar to sherry. The wine and prunes together make a surprisingly unusual and delicious combination.

1 (14-oz.) can prunes in juice
1/2 cup flour
salt and freshly ground black pepper
2 1/2 lbs. pork tenderloin, cut into
    1-inch pieces
2 tbsp. vegetable olive oil
1 large onion, thinly sliced

2 cloves garlic, crushed
3 cups sliced mushrooms
1/2 cup marsala wine
1/2 cup pork or chicken stock
1 tbsp. honey
2 tsp. dried thyme
freshly chopped parsley, to serve

Drain the prunes, reserving the juice. Remove and discard the pits. Put the flour onto a plate and season with salt and pepper. Roll the pork in the flour. Heat the oil in a large skillet over medium to high heat and quickly fry the pork pieces in two batches until nicely browned all over. With a slotted spoon, transfer the pork to a plate and set aside.

Add the onion and garlic to the skillet and cook for 3–4 minutes until softened. Transfer to the slow cooker and add the browned pork, mushrooms, marsala, stock, honey, thyme, 1/4 cup reserved prune juice, the reserved pitted prunes, and any remaining flour. Stir to combine. Cover and cook on low for 5–6 hours. When finished, taste and adjust the seasoning if necessary. If the sauce seems too thin, sprinkle 1 tablespoon flour into the pot, stir, and cook for another 10 minutes, Serve sprinkled with some chopped parsley.

Makes 6 servings

spicy pork casserole

see variations page 113

This is an excellent dish to prepare for a dinner party. The flavor is delicious, and you could serve it with either mashed or roasted potatoes. Add some green vegetables to complete the meal.

1/4 cup flour
2 tsp. curry powder
salt and freshly ground black pepper
2 lbs. lean pork, cut into 1-inch pieces
2 tbsp. vegetable oil
2 onions, finely chopped
2 cloves garlic, crushed
1 large green bell pepper, seeded and chopped

3 cups sliced mushrooms
2 leeks, washed and thinly sliced
1 (14-oz.) can diced tomatoes in juice
1 cup good-quality chicken stock
2 tsp. dried mixed Italian herbs
freshly chopped cilantro, to serve

Put the flour onto a plate, and mix in the curry powder, salt, and pepper. Roll the pork in the flour until it is well coated. Heat the vegetable oil in a large skillet, and fry the pork for 3–4 minutes, until it is nicely browned all over. Transfer with a slotted spoon to a clean plate. Add the onions and garlic to the skillet and fry over medium heat for 2 minutes until softened. Transfer to the slow cooker and add the pork, green pepper, mushrooms, leeks, tomatoes, stock, herbs, and any remaining flour. Stir well to combine. Cover and cook on low for 6–7 hours.

At the end of the cooking time, taste, and adjust the seasoning if necessary. Serve sprinkled with some chopped cilantro.

Makes 6 servings

carbonnade of beef with dumplings

see base recipe page 77

carbonnade of beef with red peppers & dumplings
Prepare the basic recipe, replacing the onions with 12 shallots, peeled and left whole, and adding 2 seeded and sliced red bell peppers.

carbonnade of beef with horseradish dumplings
Prepare the basic recipe, adding 2 tablespoons horseradish cream to the dumplings while mixing with the water.

carbonnade of beef with chorizo & dumplings
Prepare the basic recipe, adding 1 cup chopped chorizo with the onions.

carbonnade of beef with beans & dumplings
Prepare the basic recipe, adding 1/2 pound dried navy beans. Place them in a small saucepan, cover with water, bring to a boil, and simmer for 10 minutes. Drain and add to the slow cooker with the beef.

variations

beef pot roast

see base recipe page 79

beef pot roast with red cabbage & fennel
Prepare the basic recipe, adding 1 cup shredded red cabbage and
2 teaspoons fennel seeds to the slow cooker with the beef.

beef pot roast with madeira
Prepare the basic recipe, replacing 1/2 cup wine with 1/2 cup Madeira.

beef pot roast with barbecue sauce
Prepare the basic recipe, replacing 1/2 cup wine with 1/2 cup barbecue sauce
(page 94).

beef pot roast with sour cream
Prepare the basic recipe, stirring in 1/4 cup sour cream at the end of the
cooking time.

beef pot roast with wild mushrooms
Prepare the basic recipe, adding 1 cup chopped mixed wild mushrooms
1 hour before the end of the cooking time.

beef daube with herbes de provence

see base recipe page 80

hungarian goulash
Prepare the basic recipe, omitting the orange and olives. Add 1 tablespoon paprika to the skillet with the onion. Peel and dice 2 medium potatoes and gently drop them into the slow cooker before covering and cooking.

beef stew with horseradish
Prepare the basic recipe, omitting the orange zest and olives. Just before serving, stir in 2 tablespoons horseradish cream.

beef daube with kidney beans & chili
Prepare the basic recipe, omitting the orange zest and olives. Add 1 drained (14-ounce) can red kidney beans and 1 red chili, seeded and chopped, to the slow cooker with the meat.

beef daube with tomato, basil & spinach
Prepare the basic recipe, omitting the orange zest. Add 2 tablespoons freshly chopped basil to the slow cooker with the meat, and add 4 cups fresh spinach 30 minutes before the end of the cooking time. Substitute basil for the parsley, to serve.

variations

steak & guinness pudding with onion gravy

see base recipe page 82

steak & red wine pudding
Prepare the basic recipe, replacing the beer with a robust red wine.

steak & mushroom pudding
Prepare the basic recipe, adding 1/4 cup finely chopped mushrooms with the meat.

steak & leek pudding
Prepare the basic recipe, adding 1/4 cup finely chopped leeks with the meat.

steak & madeira pudding
Prepare the basic recipe, replacing the beer with Madeira and adding 1/4 cup finely chopped onion with the meat.

vegetarian pudding with onion gravy
Prepare the basic recipe, omitting the meat. Substitute mixed vegetables, all chopped to the same size. Replace the beef stock in the gravy with vegetable stock.

variations

bolognese sauce for pasta

see base recipe page 84

middle eastern mix for couscous
Prepare the basic recipe, omitting the tomato paste, red wine, carrots, and basil.
Substitute 5 tablespoons mango chutney, and add 1 seeded green pepper and
2 zucchini, both finely chopped. Add 2 teaspoons ground coriander and 4
tablespoons freshly chopped cilantro. Serve over couscous with extra cilantro.

rich beef chili
Prepare the basic recipe. Add 1 teaspoon chili powder, 2 red chilies, seeded and
finely chopped, and 4 tablespoons freshly chopped cilantro.

beef burritos
Prepare the rich beef chili variation. Put 2 tablespoons beef chili in the
middle of a tortilla, then wrap up. Spoon extra sauce on top, sprinkle with
2 tablespoons shredded cheese, and heat to melt cheese.

cottage pie
Prepare the basic recipe. Put the bolognese in a large baking dish. Cover with
mashed potatoes and let brown under the broiler.

variations

moussaka

see base recipe page 85

lamb moussaka with cinnamon
Prepare the basic recipe, replacing the beef with ground lamb, and adding 2 teaspoons ground cinnamon to the meat.

vegetarian moussaka
Prepare the basic recipe, replacing the beef with 1 1/2 pounds mixed vegetables, all chopped into the same size. Add 1 (14-ounce) can beans in chili sauce.

moussaka with chilies
Prepare the basic recipe, adding 1 teaspoon chopped mild chilies to the meat.

moussaka with dates & raisins
Prepare the basic recipe, adding 1/2 cup chopped pitted dates and 1/2 cup raisins to the meat.

moussaka with roasted vegetables & feta
Prepare the basic recipe, omitting the sliced eggplant, cheese sauce, and cheese topping. Add a layer of oven-roasted vegetables such as zucchini, red and green bell peppers, red onion, and cubed eggplant on top of the meat. Sprinkle with small cubes of feta cheese.

variations

rogan josh

see base recipe page 86

rogan josh with spinach
Prepare the basic recipe, adding 4 cups fresh spinach to the slow cooker
30 minutes before the end of the cooking time.

rogan josh with cashews
Prepare the basic recipe, replacing the almonds with 2/3 cup cashew nuts,
added to the slow cooker just before the end of the cooking time.

rogan josh with mango chutney
Prepare the basic recipe, adding 3 tablespoons mango chutney to the slow
cooker with the lamb.

rogan josh with peppers
Prepare the basic recipe, adding 2 seeded and sliced green bell peppers to the
skillet with the onion.

variations

moroccan lamb tagine

see base recipe page 88

moroccan lamb tagine with chickpeas & lemon
Prepare the basic recipe, adding 1 drained (14-ounce) can chickpeas to the slow cooker with the onion and the zest of 1 lemon an hour before the end of the cooking time.

moroccan goat tagine
Prepare the basic recipe, replacing the lamb with diced, boneless goat meat.

moroccan lamb tagine with apricots & figs
Prepare the basic recipe, adding 1/4 cup chopped dried apricots and 1/4 cup chopped dried figs to the slow cooker with the meat.

moroccan lamb tagine with harissa
Prepare the basic recipe, adding 2 tablespoons harissa paste to the slow cooker with the meat.

lamb shanks with redcurrant jelly & port

see base recipe page 89

lamb shanks with red wine & rosemary
Prepare the basic recipe, replacing 1 cup stock with 1 cup hearty red wine.
Add 1 extra teaspoon dried rosemary.

lamb shanks with roasted garlic & dried cherries
Prepare the basic recipe, adding 2 whole bulbs of garlic, roasted, and 1/2 cup
dried cherries to the slow cooker with the meat.

lamb shanks with honey & chili
Prepare the basic recipe, adding 2 tablespoons honey and 1 seeded and
finely chopped red chili pepper to the slow cooker with the meat.

lamb shanks with pancetta & beans
Prepare the basic recipe, adding 1 (14-ounce) can cannellini beans to
the slow cooker with the meat. Add 1/2 cup chopped pancetta just
before serving.

variations

lancashire hot pot with scalloped potatoes

see base recipe page 90

lancashire hot pot with sweet potatoes
Prepare the basic recipe, replacing the potatoes with sweet potatoes.

lancashire hot pot with apricots & scalloped potatoes
Prepare the basic recipe, adding 1/4 cup dried apricots to the slow cooker
with the meat before topping with the potatoes.

lamb & tomato cobbler
Prepare the basic recipe, omitting the potatoes and adding a cobbler
topping. Sift 2 cups flour, 1 teaspoon baking powder, and a pinch of salt into
a bowl. Add 1/4 cup cold butter and rub in with your fingertips until the
mixture resembles fine breadcrumbs. Mix in 1 tablespoon dried mixed herbs
and 2/3 cup milk, making a soft dough. Roll out and cut into biscuits, and
place on top of the meat about 45 minutes before the end of cooking time.

lancashire hot pot with scalloped potatoes & mushroom sauce
Prepare the basic recipe, replacing the stock with 1 (14-ounce) can
mushroom soup.

variations

lamb stew with dumplings

see base recipe page 93

lamb stew with mint dumplings
Prepare the basic recipe, replacing the mixed herbs in the dumplings with
2 tablespoons freshly chopped mint.

lamb & apricot stew with dumplings
Prepare the basic recipe, adding 1/4 cup chopped dried apricots to the slow
cooker with the meat.

lamb & madeira stew with rosemary dumplings
Prepare the basic recipe, replacing 1/2 cup chicken stock with 1/2 cup Madeira.
Replace the Italian herbs in the dumplings with 2 teaspoons dried rosemary.

lamb & bean stew with dumplings
Prepare the basic recipe, adding 1 (14-ounce) can navy beans to the slow
cooker with the meat.

lamb & mushroom stew with dumplings
Prepare the basic recipe, adding 2 cups sliced mushrooms to the slow cooker
with the meat.

variations

barbecue baby back ribs

see base recipe page 94

barbecue baby back ribs with curry seasoning
Prepare the basic recipe, replacing the Cajun seasoning with curry powder.

barbecue baby back ribs with chipotle chilies
Prepare the basic recipe, adding 2 chipotle chilies to the sauce.

sweet & spicy barbecue baby back ribs
Prepare the basic recipe, adding 2 tablespoons honey to the sauce.

oriental barbecue baby back ribs
Prepare the basic recipe, adding 2 tablespoons hoisin sauce to the barbecue sauce.

mustard barbecue baby back ribs
Prepare the basic recipe, replacing the Cajun seasoning with 2 teaspoons mustard powder.

variations

osso bucco

see base recipe page 95

osso bucco with marsala & mushrooms
Prepare the basic recipe, omitting 1/4 cup stock and the gremolata, and substituting marsala wine. Add 1 cup sliced mushrooms with the rest of the vegetables.

osso bucco with lamb shanks
Prepare the basic recipe, replacing the veal shin bone with lamb shanks.

osso bucco with turkey & cranberries
Prepare the basic recipe, replacing the veal with 3 1/2 pounds of turkey legs, and adding 1/2 cup dried cranberries. Omit the gremolata.

osso bucco with chicken & sage
Prepare the basic recipe, replacing the veal with chicken drumsticks. Omit the gremolata, and add 2 teaspoons dried sage to the slow cooker with the other ingredients.

osso bucco with red & green bell peppers
Prepare the basic recipe, adding 1 sliced red bell pepper and 1 sliced green bell pepper to the slow cooker with the onion.

variations

pork with marsala & prunes

see base recipe page 96

pork with crispy bacon & mustard
Prepare the basic recipe, adding 6 strips crisp-cooked bacon, broken into pieces, and 2 teaspoons Dijon mustard to the slow cooker with the onion.

pork with creamy white wine sauce
Prepare the basic recipe, replacing the marsala with white wine. Stir in 1/4 cup sour cream just before serving.

pork with vermouth, apples & crème fraîche
Prepare the basic recipe, replacing the marsala with dry vermouth. Add 2, peeled, cored, and chopped apples to the slow cooker with the meat, and stir in 1/4 cup crème fraîche just before serving.

pork with marsala & prunes with apple dumplings
Prepare the basic recipe. Make apple dumplings, following the recipe for the dumplings on page 77, but adding 2 tablespoons applesauce with the water when mixing. Add to the slow cooker 20 minutes before the end of cooking time.

spicy pork casserole

see base recipe page 98

spicy pork with chickpeas, lentils & vegetables
Prepare the basic recipe, adding 1 drained (14-ounce) can chickpeas, 1/4 cup
puy lentils, and 2 peeled and chopped carrots to the slow cooker with the
meat. Replace the cilantro with parsley.

spicy pork with apricots, raisins & dates
Prepare the basic recipe, omitting the green peppers and adding 1/4 cup
chopped dried apricots, 1/4 cup raisins, and 1/4 cup fresh or dried pitted dates
to the slow cooker with the meat.

spicy pork with celery & pancetta
Prepare the basic recipe, adding 2 sliced celery stalks to the slow cooker with
the meat, and 1/4 cup chopped pancetta just before serving.

spicy pork with leeks & ale
Prepare the basic recipe, replacing the chicken stock with dark beer. Replace
the cilantro with parsley.

poultry & game

Poultry is lean, healthy, and one of the easiest and most versatile meats to cook in the slow cooker. Game is also a good choice, as the slow cooker will tenderize and improve the cheaper meats. Use a strong stock to improve flavor.

chicken chorizo & rice

see variations page 138

This is sometimes called Spanish rice because it contains spicy sausage and olives. The flavor from the chorizo permeates the rice and the chicken, and the result is delicious.

10–12 skinless and boneless chicken thighs
salt and freshly ground black pepper
2 tbsp. olive oil
2 large onions, finely chopped
3 cloves garlic, crushed
2 tbsp. tomato paste
1/4 cup sun-dried tomatoes
1 tsp. ground turmeric
1 tsp. smoked paprika

1/2 lb. chorizo sausage, cut into 1-inch pieces
1/2 cup white wine
1 1/2 cups good-quality chicken stock
2 (14-oz.) cans chopped tomatoes in juice
2 cups parboiled rice (boiled for 5 minutes)
1 red bell pepper, seeded and sliced
1 cup frozen peas
1/4 cup pitted black olives
1/2 large orange, cut into wedges
3 tbsp. freshly chopped parsley

Trim away as much fat as possible from the chicken thighs and check there are no tiny bits of bone left. Cut each one in half, and season with salt and freshly ground black pepper. In a large skillet, heat the oil and fry the chicken for about 5 minutes or until nicely browned all over. Transfer with a slotted spoon to a clean plate. Add the onion and garlic to the pan and fry for 5 minutes until softened, then add the tomato paste, sun-dried tomatoes, turmeric, and paprika. Cook for 2 minutes. Add the wine and simmer for a few minutes until slightly reduced, scraping the bottom of the pan to deglaze. Transfer to the slow cooker, add the chicken thighs, chorizo, chicken stock, tomatoes, rice, and pepper. Cook on low for 5–6 hours. Thirty minutes before the end of the cooking time, taste and adjust the seasoning if necessary, and add the frozen peas, olives, orange wedges, and parsley.

Makes 6 servings

chicken shiraz with ginger

see variations page 139

Shiraz (also known as Syrah) is a hearty and spicy, fine, dark red wine with intense flavors.

6 strips smoked bacon, chopped
2 cups sliced mushrooms
2 carrots, peeled and sliced
2 stalks celery, sliced
2 sprigs fresh rosemary
2 sprigs fresh thyme
10–12 skinless and boneless chicken thighs
1/4 cup flour
salt and freshly ground black pepper
1 large onion, coarsely chopped

1 tsp. finely chopped gingerroot
3 cloves garlic, crushed
2 tbsp. tomato paste
1 1/2 cups Shiraz or Burgundy wine
1 cup good-quality chicken stock
1 chicken stock cube
2 tbsp. brandy
12 shallots, peeled and left whole
2 tsp. cornstarch mixed with a little
    water (optional)
freshly chopped parsley, to serve

Put the mushrooms, carrots, celery, and herbs into the slow cooker. In a large skillet, dry-fry the bacon until browned and crispy. Remove, and drain on paper towels. Set aside. Put the flour onto a plate, add salt and pepper, and dredge the chicken to coat it all over. Fry the chicken in the bacon drippings in the skillet until nicely browned all over, and transfer to the slow cooker. Add the onion, ginger, and garlic to the skillet. Fry until softened, about 5 minutes. Transfer to the slow cooker. In a medium bowl, mix the tomato paste with the wine, stock, stock cube, and brandy, and add to the slow cooker with the remaining flour and the shallots. Stir to combine all ingredients. Cover and cook on low for 8 hours. Before serving, taste and adjust the seasoning if necessary. Remove the herb sprigs if you can. If the sauce seems thin, add the cornstarch mixed with a little water, stir well, and leave for 10 minutes. Serve sprinkled with freshly chopped parsley.

Makes 6 servings

chicken with satay sauce

see variations page 140

Generally chicken satay is served as a kebab with a satay dip. Cooking it in the slow cooker makes a delicious change.

4 skinless and boneless chicken breasts
2 tbsp. Cajun seasoning
2 tbsp. vegetable oil
1 sweet potato, finely diced
freshly ground black pepper
1 large onion, coarsely chopped
2 cloves garlic, crushed
2 tsp. ground cumin

2 tsp. ground coriander
1 tsp. mild chili powder
1 cup coconut milk
4 tbsp. smooth peanut butter
3 tbsp. soy sauce
1 tbsp. lemon juice
1/2 cup water
freshly chopped cilantro, to serve (optional)

Sprinkle the chicken breasts with Cajun seasoning. Heat the oil in a large skillet over medium to high heat, and sear the chicken breasts until nicely browned all over. Transfer to the slow cooker and add the diced sweet potato. Season with black pepper. Lower the heat under the skillet and add the onion and garlic. Cook for 5 minutes or until softened. Add the cumin, coriander, and chili powder, and cook for 1 minute. Add mixture to the slow cooker.
In a medium bowl, add the coconut milk to the peanut butter a little at a time, stirring to combine. Stir in the soy sauce, lemon juice, and water, and transfer to the slow cooker. Stir to combine everything together, cover, and cook on low for 4 hours. To serve, adjust the seasoning as needed and sprinkle with cilantro, if using.

Makes 4 servings

thai red chicken curry

see variations page 141

When you are seeding and chopping red chilies, wear rubber gloves and protective glasses. It is very painful to get the juice on your face or in your eyes. This curry dish is delicious over rice.

for the curry paste
2 shallots, coarsely chopped
1 stalk lemongrass, trimmed and chopped
3 red chilies, seeded and chopped
1 (1-inch) piece gingerroot, peeled,
    and finely chopped
zest and juice of 1 lime
1 tbsp. fish sauce (or soy sauce)

1 tsp. ground coriander
1 tsp. ground cumin
1 tsp. ground white pepper
1 tsp. paprika
for the curry dish
1 tbsp. vegetable oil
6 skinless and boneless chicken breasts
2 1/4 cups thick coconut milk (not light)

To make the curry paste, put all the ingredients in a food processor. Process until you have a smooth paste.

In a large skillet, heat the vegetable oil, add the chicken, and fry for a few minutes until the pieces are browned all over. Lift out with a slotted spoon and transfer to the slow cooker. Add the curry paste to the skillet and fry for 2 minutes. Slowly add the coconut milk, stirring continually and scraping the bottom of the skillet to deglaze. Transfer the sauce to the slow cooker, cover, and cook on low for 5–6 hours. Serve over rice.

Makes 6 servings

chicken dhansak

see variations page 142

This is a Persian curry made with lentils and spices. You can make it with lamb or beef, but it is particularly good made with chicken.

10–12 skinless and boneless chicken thighs
2 tbsp. curry powder
2 tbsp. vegetable oil
2 red onions
3 cloves garlic, crushed
2 tsp. ground turmeric
2 tsp. ground coriander
1 tsp. chili powder

1 tsp. ground cumin
1 tsp. sugar
1 (14-oz.) can chopped tomatoes in juice
1 tbsp. soy sauce
3/4 cup dried lentils, rinsed
3/4 cup good-quality chicken stock
1 red chili pepper, seeded and chopped
1/4 cup freshly chopped cilantro

Trim the chicken thighs of any visible fat and check that no tiny bits of bone are left. Cut each one in half, put on a plate, and sprinkle with 2 tablespoons curry powder, turning the chicken around to coat evenly. In a large skillet, heat the vegetable oil, and fry the chicken in batches until it is nicely browned all over. Transfer with a slotted spoon to a plate, and set aside. Add the onions and garlic to the pan, and cook over medium heat for 5 minutes until softened. Add the turmeric, coriander, chili powder, cumin, and sugar, and cook for 2 minutes. Stirring continually, add the tomatoes and the soy sauce to the pan, and heat, scraping the bottom of the pan to deglaze. Transfer to the slow cooker. Put the lentils in medium saucepan, add water to cover by about 2 inches, and bring to a boil. Simmer for 10 minutes. Drain, and add to the slow cooker along with the chicken and chicken stock. Stir well. Cover and cook on low for 5–6 hours. Just before serving, add the chopped red chili and chopped fresh cilantro.

Makes 6 servings

turkey in creamy cider sauce

see variations page 143

This is a mild, creamy sauce. The cream is added at the end, as dairy products do not slow-cook very successfully (they tend to separate).

4 tbsp. butter
8–10 shallots, coarsely chopped
4 stalks celery, sliced
6 turkey breast fillets
1/4 cup flour
salt and freshly ground black pepper
2 cups sliced mushrooms
1 tsp. dried tarragon leaves

4 apples, cored and cut into wedges
    (no need to peel)
1 cup apple cider or apple juice
1/4 cup good-quality chicken stock
1 chicken stock cube
1/3 cup heavy cream
3 tbsp. freshly chopped chives, to serve

Heat 2 tablespoons butter in a large skillet, add the shallots and celery, and cook for 5 minutes until softened. Lift out with a slotted spoon and transfer to the slow cooker. Dredge the turkey breast fillets with flour seasoned with salt and freshly ground black pepper. Add the turkey fillets to the skillet and brown all over. Add the mushrooms and tarragon to the slow cooker and place the browned turkey on top. In the skillet, melt the remaining butter, then add the apple wedges. Cook for a few minutes until nicely browned, and transfer to the slow cooker with any remaining flour. Add the cider or apple juice, chicken stock, and stock cube to the slow cooker, stir, cover, and cook on low for 6–7 hours.

At the end of the cooking time, transfer the turkey fillets to a plate and keep warm. Add the heavy cream to the sauce. Stir to combine. Taste and adjust the seasoning as needed. Serve the turkey with the sauce, sprinkled with chopped chives.

Makes 6 servings

sausage-stuffed chicken breasts & ratatouille

see variations page 144

Chicken is stuffed with sausage and basil, wrapped in parchment paper, and rested on top of hearty ratatouille. All you need to complete the meal is some crusty bread.

1/2 lb. good-quality sausage meat (such as mild Italian sausage)
1 tbsp. freshly chopped basil
4 skinless and boneless chicken breasts
2 tbsp. extra-virgin olive oil
salt and freshly ground black pepper
dried red pepper flakes

for the ratatouille
1 large red onion, cut into large chunks
1 eggplant, cut into large cubes
3 zucchini, sliced into chunks
1 red bell pepper, seeded and cut bite-size
1 green bell pepper, seeded and cut bite-size
3 tbsp. freshly chopped basil
4 tbsp. tomato paste
salt and freshly ground black pepper

Mix the sausage meat with the basil. Cut a pocket in each chicken breast and stuff each with a quarter of the sausage. Place each breast on a large square of parchment or waxed paper, brush each breast with oil, and season with salt and pepper. Sprinkle with some red pepper flakes. Wrap each chicken breast into a parcel and secure with string tied in a bow. Set aside. Make the ratatouille by mixing all the vegetables, basil, and tomato paste together in the slow cooker. Season with salt and pepper. Place the chicken parcels on top, cover, and cook on low for 10 hours. To serve, unwrap the chicken parcels and serve with the ratatouille.

Makes 4 servings

turkey & cranberry chili

see variations page 145

Although this chili is made with turkey, which is healthier, I like it to taste as much like beef as possible, so I use beef stock rather than chicken and add some Worcestershire sauce. Turkey is quite a bland tasting meat, so lots of spices and cranberries add a good depth of flavor.

1 tbsp. vegetable oil
1 1/2 lbs. ground turkey
1 large onion, finely chopped
2 cloves garlic, crushed
2 tsp. dried mixed Italian herbs
1 tsp. chili powder
1 tsp. ground cumin
1 tsp. ground coriander
1 medium potato, peeled and diced
2 tsp. currant jelly
2 tbsp. tomato paste

1 tbsp. Worcestershire sauce
2 cups sliced mushrooms
1/4 cup sliced wild mushrooms, such as shiitake
1 1/2 cups good-quality beef stock
1 beef stock cube
1/3 cup red wine
1 red chili, seeded and finely chopped
2/3 cup dried cranberries
3 tbsp. freshly chopped cilantro

In a large skillet, heat the oil, and brown the turkey, stirring to break up the lumps. Add the onion and garlic, and cook for 5 minutes until softened. Add the Italian herbs, chili powder, cumin, coriander, currant jelly, tomato paste, and Worcestershire sauce. Cook for 1 minute. Transfer to the slow cooker and add the mushrooms, beef stock, and red wine. Stir to combine the ingredients. Cover and cook on low for 6 hours. Just before serving, taste and adjust the seasoning as needed, and stir in the red chili, cranberries, and cilantro.

Makes 6 servings

duck with dark cherry sauce

see variations page 146

Dry-frying the duck breasts before adding them to the sauce gets rid of quite a bit of fat from underneath the skin. The sweetness of the cherries contrast beautifully with the strong duck flavor.

2 large duck breasts, skin on
salt and freshly ground black pepper
2 shallots, finely chopped
1 cup port wine
1 cup good-quality chicken stock
few sprigs fresh thyme

1/2 lb. fresh or canned dark cherries, pitted
   and halved
2 tbsp. black cherry preserves
2 tsp. cornstarch mixed with a little water
   (optional)
freshly chopped parsley, to serve (optional)

Slice each duck breast in half and season with salt and pepper. Heat a large skillet until it is good and hot, and dry-fry the duck, skin-side down. Leave it in the pan without moving it around for 4–5 minutes, until most of the fat from under the skin has rendered down and the skin is crisp and golden. Turn the duck over and brown the other side for 2–3 minutes. Transfer to the slow cooker. Pour off most of the fat from the skillet, add the shallots, and cook for 1–2 minutes. Add the port and heat, scraping the bottom of the pan to deglaze. Add the stock, thyme, cherries, and cherry preserves, stirring continuously. Transfer to the slow cooker. Cook on low for 5 hours.

Before serving, taste and adjust the seasoning if needed. If the sauce seems a little thin, thicken it with a little diluted cornstarch, and leave it in the slow cooker for another 10 minutes. Serve sprinkled with parsley, if using.

Makes 4 servings

pot-roasted pheasant

see variations page 147

You can use pheasant or grouse, depending upon your personal preference and what is available.

2 pheasants, plucked, gutted, and prepared
salt and freshly ground black pepper
2 tbsp. vegetable oil
2 strips bacon, chopped
1 large onion, coarsely chopped
4 cloves garlic, crushed
2 stalks celery, sliced
1 lb. carrots, peeled and sliced

2 tbsp. fresh tarragon leaves
2/3 cup dry white wine
1 chicken stock cube
1/4 cup chicken stock
2 tsp. cornstarch mixed with a little water
2 tbsp. heavy cream
freshly chopped parsley, to serve

Season the pheasants with plenty of salt and pepper. Heat the oil in a large skillet and, one at a time, evenly brown the pheasants on both sides. Set aside. Add the bacon, onion, garlic, and celery to the skillet and cook for 5 minutes, then transfer to the slow cooker with the carrots. Add the pheasants with the tarragon, white wine, chicken stock cube, and stock. Cover and cook on low for 6 hours.

At the end of the cooking time, lift out the pheasants and keep warm. Skim off any fat from the surface of the stock, then thicken the sauce with a little cornstarch mixed with cold water. Stir the heavy cream into the sauce, taste, and adjust the seasoning if necessary. Return the pheasants to the sauce, and serve sprinkled with freshly chopped parsley.

Makes 4 servings

rabbit cacciatore

see variations page 148

Rabbit is very lean meat and lower in cholesterol than chicken or turkey. It is almost always sold skinned and cleaned, and either cut-up or left whole. One rabbit weighing about 3 pounds will serve 4 people. This recipe works well with chicken, if you prefer.

1 (3-lb.) rabbit, cut into 6 pieces
salt and freshly ground black pepper
2 tbsp. olive oil
1 medium onion, finely chopped
2 cloves garlic, crushed
2 green bell peppers, seeded and thinly sliced
1 (14-oz.) can chopped tomatoes in juice

2 cups sliced mushrooms
1 cup dry white wine
2 chicken stock cubes
1 tbsp. dried mixed Italian herbs
1 tsp. anchovy paste
freshly chopped parsley, to serve
shredded Parmesan cheese, to serve

Season the rabbit generously with salt and pepper. In a large skillet, heat the oil and fry the rabbit pieces until they are nicely browned all over. Transfer the rabbit with a slotted spoon to a plate and set aside. Add the onion and garlic to the skillet and cook over medium heat for 5 minutes, or until softened. Transfer to the slow cooker, and add the rabbit, peppers, tomatoes, mushrooms, wine, stock cubes, herbs, and anchovy paste. Stir to combine everything together. Cover and cook on low for 6–7 hours.

To serve, taste and adjust seasoning if necessary. Serve sprinkled with parsley and Parmesan cheese.

Makes 4 servings

venison in rich gravy

see variations page 149

Venison is a very low-fat meat. If you want to lower the fat content of this dish even more, leave out the bacon and use 2 tablespoons olive oil to fry the venison.

1 1/2 lbs. venison
1/4 cup flour
salt and freshly ground black pepper
6 strips bacon, chopped
1 tbsp. olive oil
14 small shallots, peeled and left whole

1 lb. celeriac, peeled and diced
2 cups good-quality beef or game stock
2 beef stock cubes
2 tbsp. Worcestershire sauce
2 tsp. juniper berries, crushed
freshly chopped parsley, to serve

Cut the venison into cubes. Put the flour on a plate and season with salt and pepper. Roll the venison in the flour to coat it all over. Heat a large skillet and dry-fry the bacon until it is nicely browned. Remove with a slotted spoon to drain on paper towels. Pour off most of the fat from the skillet, add the venison in batches, and brown it all over. Remove with a slotted spoon and transfer it to the slow cooker. If necessary, add a little olive oil to the skillet and fry the shallots and celeriac until they start to color. Add to the venison in the slow cooker. Add the remainder of the flour, bacon, stock, stock cubes, Worcestershire sauce, and crushed juniper berries. Cover, and cook on low for 6–7 hours. Before serving, taste and adjust the seasoning if necessary. Serve sprinkled with chopped parsley.

Makes 6 servings

venison sausages in brown ale

see variations page 150

If venison sausages are hard to find, use any premium quality fresh sausages. The beer makes a rich and hearty a that complements the sausages beautifully.

2 tbsp. vegetable oil
8 venison sausages
1 large onion, thinly sliced
2 tsp. flour
2 tsp. Dijon mustard
2 tsp. Worcestershire sauce
1 cup beef stock

1 beef stock cube
1 cup dark ale
2 tsp. dried thyme
2 bay leaves
salt and freshly ground black pepper
2 tsp. cornstarch mixed with a little water

In a large skillet, heat the oil over high heat and fry the sausages until they are browned but not cooked through. Transfer with a slotted spoon to a plate and set aside. Add the onions to the skillet, turn the heat down to medium, and cook the onions until they are softened and lightly colored. Stir in the flour and mustard and cook for 2 minutes, then add the Worcestershire sauce. Stirring continuously, gradually add the stock, stock cube, and ale. Bring to a boil, then transfer to the slow cooker with the herbs. Add the sausages, season with salt and pepper, cover, and cook on low for 6–7 hours.

Before serving, taste and adjust the seasoning if needed. If the sauce seems thin, thicken with diluted cornstarch and let stand for another 10 minutes.

Makes 4 servings

wild boar & pork with rioja

see variations page 151

If you cannot find wild boar, just use pork shoulder.

1 lb. wild boar for stewing, trimmed of fat
1 lb. pork shoulder, trimmed of fat
for the marinade
1 small onion, finely chopped
1 stalk celery, thinly sliced
2 cloves garlic, crushed
4 fresh sage leaves
1 sprig rosemary
2 bay leaves
2 tsp. dried thyme
2-3 cloves
2 tbsp. red wine vinegar
2 tbsp. Rioja red wine
2 tbsp. olive oil
1 tsp. salt
2 tsp. freshly ground black pepper

for the stew
1/4 cup flour
salt and freshly ground black pepper
2 tbsp. olive oil
1 large onion, thinly sliced
2 cloves garlic, crushed
1 cup good-quality beef stock
1 or 2 beef stock cubes
1/2 cup hearty red wine
2 tomatoes, chopped
1 tbsp. tomato paste
2 cups sliced mushrooms
2 bay leaves
2 tsp. dried rosemary
2 tsp. cornstarch mixed with a little water
1/2 cup fresh or frozen blueberries
freshly chopped parsley, to serve

Cut the meat into 2-inch pieces. Combine the ingredients for the marinade, add the meat, and stir to mix well. Cover and refrigerate for 24 hours.

Before cooking, drain the meat and pat dry with paper towels. Season the flour with salt and pepper, and coat the meat. In a large skillet, fry the meat in batches until nicely browned, remove with a slotted spoon, and set aside. Add the onion and garlic to the pan, and cook

gently until softened and lightly colored. Add the remaining flour to the skillet, stir, then gradually add the stock, stock cubes, red wine, tomatoes, and tomato paste. Stirring continuously to deglaze the pan, bring to a boil and simmer for 1 minute. Transfer to the slow cooker and add the meat, mushrooms, and herbs. Cover and cook on low for 7–8 hours. When done, adjust the seasoning if needed. If the sauce is thin, thicken it with the cornstarch mixture, stir well, add the blueberries, and cook for 10 minutes more. Serve sprinkled with parsley.

Makes 6 servings

variations

chicken, chorizo & rice

see base recipe page 115

oriental chicken & rice
Prepare the basic recipe, omitting the chorizo, tomato paste, turmeric, paprika, olives, and orange. Add 1 teaspoon Chinese five-spice powder, 1 cup snow peas, and 1 cup baby corn. In the last half hour, add 1/2 cup drained canned pineapple chunks and 1/2 cup cooked shrimp.

barbecue chicken & rice with honey
Prepare the basic recipe, omitting the chorizo, turmeric, olives, and orange. Add 1 teaspoon barbecue seasoning, 3 tablespoons barbecue sauce, and 2 tablespoons honey with the white wine.

turkish chicken & rice
Prepare the basic recipe, omitting the chorizo, paprika, turmeric, and orange. Substitute 1 teaspoon each ground coriander and cumin and 10 stems saffron ground with 1 teaspoon boiling water. In last half hour, add 1 cup raisins and 1/2 cup whole almonds.

caribbean chicken & rice
Prepare the basic recipe, omitting the chorizo, paprika, olives, and orange. Add 1 teaspoon each ground coriander and cinnamon and 1/2 teaspoon each ground cumin and ginger with the turmeric.

chicken shiraz with ginger

see base recipe page 117

chicken with wine & cream sauce
Prepare the basic recipe, replacing ginger and Shiraz with white wine. Before serving, stir in 3 tablespoons heavy cream.

chicken marsala with basil
Prepare the base recipe, replacing ginger and Shiraz with marsala wine. Omit the rosemary and thyme. Replace the parsley with 1/2 cup freshly chopped basil.

chicken in white wine & tarragon
Prepare the basic recipe, replacing ginger, Shiraz, rosemary, and thyme with white wine and 2 tablespoons fresh tarragon leaves.

chicken marengo
Prepare the basic recipe, omitting Shiraz, ginger, and shallots. Substitute 1 cup white wine and 1 large chopped onion. An hour before the end of cooking time, remove the chicken from the slow cooker and, keeping the sauce, strain and discard the vegetables. Put the sauce back into the slow cooker, thicken with cornstarch, add the mushrooms, and return the chicken to the sauce. Cover and cook for the last hour.

variations

chicken with satay sauce

see base recipe page 118

chicken & mushrooms with satay sauce
Prepare the basic recipe, adding 3 cups sliced mushrooms and 1 (14-ounce) can mushroom soup.

chicken & peppers with satay sauce
Prepare the basic recipe, adding 2 sliced green bell peppers with the onions.

chicken satay with water chestnuts & cashews
Prepare the basic recipe, adding 1 cup sliced water chestnuts and 1/2 cup cashews in the last half hour of cooking.

chicken satay with pineapple & pine nuts
Prepare the basic recipe, adding 1 cup drained canned pineapple chunks and 1/4 cup pine nuts in the last half hour of cooking.

chicken & corn with almond-satay sauce
Prepare the basic recipe, adding about 6-8 baby corn with the onions, and 1/4 cup whole almonds in the last half hour of cooking.

thai red chicken curry

see base recipe page 121

thai red chicken curry with green beans
Prepare the basic recipe, adding 1 cup green beans to the slow cooker at the same time as the coconut milk.

thai red chicken curry with red bell peppers & almonds
Prepare the basic recipe, adding 2 sliced red bell peppers to the slow cooker with the coconut milk. Sprinkle some toasted sliced almonds with the cilantro over the curry to serve.

thai red chicken curry with basil & coconut cream
Prepare the basic recipe, omitting the cilantro. Add 1/4 cup freshly chopped basil and 1/4 cup coconut cream just before serving.

thai red chicken curry with potatoes & cashews
Prepare the basic recipe, adding 1 peeled and diced large potato to the slow cooker with the coconut milk, and 1/2 cup cashews just before serving.

thai red chicken curry with bok choy & pine nuts
Prepare the basic recipe, adding 2 chopped bok choy and 1/4 cup pine nuts 1 hour before the end of the cooking time.

variations

chicken dhansak

see base recipe page 122

chicken dhansak with spinach
Prepare the basic recipe. Thirty minutes before serving, add 4 cups fresh spinach to the curry, stir to combine, and finish cooking.

chicken dhansak with red & green bell peppers
Prepare the basic recipe, adding 1 red and 1 green bell pepper, sliced, to the slow cooker with the chicken.

chicken dhansak with mushrooms
Prepare the basic recipe, adding 2 cups sliced mushrooms to the slow cooker with the chicken.

chicken dhansak with mixed vegetables
Prepare the basic recipe, adding 1/4 cup frozen peas, 1/4 cup sliced carrots, and 1 peeled and diced potato to the slow cooker with the chicken.

chicken dhansak with quick pilau rice
Prepare the basic recipe, and serve with pilau rice. Put 1 1/2 cups basmati rice in a large saucepan and cover with water. Bring to a boil, cover, and cook for 10 minutes over medium heat. Drain the rice and put it back in the saucepan. Stir in 1 teaspoon ground cumin and 2 shallots, chopped and fried in a little oil.

variations

turkey in creamy cider sauce

see base recipe page 123

turkey in spicy cider sauce
Prepare the basic recipe, adding 2 teaspoons garam masala or ground cumin to the skillet with the shallots.

turkey in creamy cider sauce with almonds
Prepare the basic recipe, adding 1/2 cup sliced almonds to the slow cooker with the apples.

turkey in creamy white wine sauce
Prepare the basic recipe, replacing the cider or apple juice with white wine.

turkey in creamy cider sauce with peaches
Prepare the basic recipe, omitting the apples. Add 1 cup sliced fresh or canned peaches to the slow cooker with the stock.

turkey in creamy cider sauce with leeks & thyme
Prepare the basic recipe, replacing the tarragon with 2 teaspoons dried thyme. Add 2 sliced leeks to the skillet with the shallots and celery.

variations

sausage-stuffed chicken breasts & ratatouille

see base recipe page 124

sausage & sage-stuffed chicken breasts with ratatouille
Prepare the basic recipe, replacing the basil with 1 tablespoon dried sage
and 1 chopped shallot, fried in a little olive oil.

sausage & chestnut-stuffed chicken breasts with ratatouille
Prepare the basic recipe, replacing the basil with 2 tablespoons chopped
cooked fresh or canned chestnuts.

spicy sausage & cheese-stuffed chicken breasts with ratatouille
Prepare the basic recipe, using hot Italian sausage meat mixed with
2 tablespoons shredded cheddar cheese.

sausage, rice & raisin-stuffed chicken breasts with spicy ratatouille
Prepare the basic recipe, omitting the basil and half the sausage meat.
Substitute 3 tablespoons cooked white basmati rice and 1 tablespoon
raisins. Add 1 finely chopped hot red chili to the ratatouille.

sausage & cranberry-stuffed chicken breasts with ratatouille
Prepare the basic recipe, replacing the basil with 2 tablespoons
dried cranberries.

variations

turkey & cranberry chili

see base recipe page 126

turkey & cranberry chili with kidney beans
Prepare the basic recipe, adding 1 drained (14-ounce) can red kidney beans in chili sauce to the slow cooker with the turkey.

turkey & cranberry chili with red & green bell peppers
Prepare the basic recipe, adding 1 red and 1 green bell pepper, sliced, to the skillet with the Italian herbs and chili powder.

turkey & cranberry chili with jalapeños & nachos
Prepare the basic recipe, adding 1 or 2 (or to taste) seeded and chopped jalapeño peppers to the skillet with the onions. Serve over nachos, sprinkled with shredded cheddar cheese and with a side of sour cream and tomato salsa.

turkey & cranberry chili with hot dogs
Prepare the basic recipe, adding 4 hot dogs, sliced into 1-inch pieces, 30 minutes before serving.

turkey & cranberry chili with avocado salsa
Prepare the basic recipe. Serve with avocado salsa made by mixing 1 chopped ripe avocado with 2 chopped tomatoes, 2 tablespoons freshly chopped cilantro, and 1 tablespoon extra-virgin olive oil.

variations

duck with dark cherry sauce

see base recipe page 127

retro duck & orange sauce
Prepare the basic recipe, omitting port, half the chicken stock, thyme, cherries, and preserves. Substitute 1 orange, rind removed and sliced into strips, pith removed and flesh broken into segments, 1 cup red wine, 1/2 cup freshly squeezed orange juice, and 2 tablespoons honey, added with the chicken stock to the slow cooker.

duck in duck sauce (fresh plum sauce)
Instead of the basic recipe, after frying the duck, put 1 cup chopped plums, 1 cup peeled, chopped apples, and 1/2 cup peeled, chopped pears in the slow cooker. Sprinkle with 1/4 cup packed dark brown sugar, 1/2 teaspoon crushed garlic, and 2 teaspoons soy sauce. Stir, place duck on top, cover, and cook on low for 5 hours. Before serving, blend sauce until smooth.

duck with peppercorns & brandy
Prepare the basic recipe, omitting port, stock, thyme, cherries, and preserves. Add 1 cup white wine, 1 chicken stock cube, and 2 more shallots to the skillet. Add 4 tablespoons brandy and 4 tablespoons whole green peppercorns (or 1 tablespoon black peppercorns, crushed) to the slow cooker. Before serving, stir in 1/2 cup heavy cream.

pot-roasted pheasant

see base recipe page 128

pot-roasted pheasant with spinach & pine nuts
Prepare the basic recipe. An hour before the end of the cooking time, add 4 cups chopped fresh spinach and 1/2 cup pine nuts.

pot-roasted pheasant with fennel & pancetta
Prepare the basic recipe, adding 2 teaspoons fennel seeds to the skillet with the onion. Add 1/2 cup roughly chopped pancetta to the slow cooker 30 minutes before serving.

pot-roasted pheasant with barley & root vegetables
Prepare the basic recipe, adding 1/4 cup barley and 2 cups chopped mixed root vegetables to the slow cooker with the pheasants.

pot-roasted pheasant with chestnuts & madeira
Prepare the basic recipe, replacing the white wine with Madeira. Add 1 cup cooked fresh or canned chestnuts to the slow cooker 30 minutes before the end of the cooking time.

variations

rabbit cacciatore

see base recipe page 131

rabbit cacciatore with chianti
Prepare the basic recipe, replacing the white wine with Chianti.

rabbit & sausage cacciatore with basil
Prepare the basic recipe, adding 1 cup ground Italian sausage to the skillet
with the onion. Just before serving, add 2 tablespoons freshly chopped basil.

rabbit cacciatore with cannellini beans
Prepare the basic recipe, adding 1 cup canned cannellini beans to the slow
cooker with the rabbit.

rabbit & pancetta cacciatore
Prepare the basic recipe, adding 1 cup chopped pancetta to the slow cooker
30 minutes before the end of the cooking time.

rabbit cacciatore with lentils & oregano
Prepare the basic recipe, adding 1 cup canned puy (French) lentils to
the slow cooker with the rabbit, and replacing the Italian herbs with
1 tablespoon dried oregano.

venison in rich gravy

see base recipe page 132

venison in port & currant sauce

Prepare the basic recipe, replacing 1/4 cup stock with 1/4 cup port wine and adding 3 tablespoons currant jelly to the gravy.

venison, sage & chestnuts in rich gravy

Prepare the basic recipe, adding 1 tablespoon dried sage to the gravy. Add 1 cup fresh or canned cooked chestnuts to the slow cooker 30 minutes before the end of the cooking time.

venison in beer & brown sugar gravy

Prepare the basic recipe, replacing 1 cup stock with 1 cup dark beer. Add 2 tablespoons dark brown sugar to the gravy.

venison & potato goulash

Prepare the basic recipe, adding 1 peeled and diced large potato and 2 tablespoons paprika to the slow cooker with the meat.

venison in tapenade gravy

Prepare the basic recipe, adding 2 tablespoons prepared tapenade to the slow cooker with the meat.

venison sausages in brown ale

see base recipe page 135

venison sausages in espagnole sauce
Prepare the basic recipe, omitting the mustard, beer, 1/2 cup beef stock, and bay leaves. To the onion in the skillet, add 2 cloves garlic and 2 cups sliced mushrooms. Add 1 (14-ounce) can chopped tomatoes in juice and 2 tablespoons each of sherry and ketchup with the rest of the ingredients in the skillet. Transfer to the slow cooker and add a bouquet garni, which you should remove before serving.

venison sausages & mushrooms in red wine
Prepare the basic recipe, replacing the beer with red wine. Add 2 cups sliced mushrooms to the slow cooker with the sausages.

venison sausages, vegetables & potatoes in brown ale
Prepare the basic recipe, adding 3 peeled and sliced carrots, 1 peeled and diced small butternut squash, and 1 peeled and diced white turnip. Add an extra 1/4 cup stock, and put a layer of peeled and sliced potatoes on top.

wild boar & pork with rioja

see base recipe page 136

wild boar & pork with rum & oranges

Prepare the basic recipe, omitting the blueberries, and adding the rind and juice of 1 orange to the slow cooker with the mushrooms and herbs. Add 1/4 cup of dark rum to the stew 30 minutes before the end of the cooking time.

wild boar & pork with madeira & bacon

Prepare the basic recipe, omitting the blueberries, and replacing the red wine with Madeira. An hour before the end of the cooking time, add 6 strips of bacon, cooked until crispy, and chopped.

wild boar & pork with ginger wine & peaches

Prepare the basic recipe, omitting the blueberries, and replacing the red wine with ginger wine. Add 1 (14-ounce) can sliced peaches, drained, to the slow cooker.

wild boar & pork with prunes

Prepare the basic recipe, omitting the blueberries and the red wine, and adding 1 (14-ounce) can of prunes, pitted. Just before serving, add 1/4 cup pickled walnuts (if you can find them).

vegetable mains

Slow cookers are mostly associated with meat stews and casseroles. However, with or without meat, it is equally possible to produce delicious meals to captivate even the most discerning meat eater or vegetarian.

turkish stuffed eggplant

see variations page 167

Traditionally called imam bayildi, this takes its name from the Imam, or Muslim holy man. He is said to have swooned with pleasure, or from overeating, after being served this dish.

2 small eggplants
2 tbsp. olive oil
1 large onion, finely chopped
2 cloves garlic, crushed
4 tomatoes, skinned, seeded, and chopped

1 tsp. ground cinnamon
1 tsp. sugar
4 tbsp. freshly chopped parsley
3 tbsp. pine nuts
salt and freshly ground black pepper

Cut the eggplants in half, leaving the stalk intact, if you can. Scoop out most of the flesh, leaving a thin border around the edge. Set the skins aside. Chop up the flesh. In a large skillet, heat the oil, and fry the onion and garlic for 5 minutes, or until softened. Add the tomatoes, cinnamon, sugar, parsley, and pine nuts. Stir in the chopped eggplant flesh and pile the mixture into the eggplant shells. Season with salt and freshly ground black pepper.

Place the eggplants on a rack in the slow cooker. If you do not have a rack, crunch up some aluminum foil and use that instead. Place the eggplants on top, and pour in enough hot water to come about 1 inch up the sides. Cover, and cook on low for 3–4 hours. Serve 2 halves per person.

Makes 2 servings

hungarian vegetable stew

see variations page 168

This hearty stew of beans, potatoes, and lots of other vegetables blends the subtle flavors of bay and paprika with chili pepper and Hungarian red wine. The beans add protein to the stew.

1 large red bell pepper, seeded and diced
3 medium potatoes, peeled and diced
3 carrots, peeled and diced
1 turnip or parsnip, peeled and diced
1/2 rutabaga, peeled and diced
1 (14-oz.) can cannellini beans, drained (or any white beans)
1 (14-oz.) can chopped tomatoes in juice
1 large red onion, finely chopped
5 shallots, peeled
3 cloves garlic
2 tsp. paprika

2 bay leaves
1 cup hearty Hungarian red wine (or any hearty red wine)
1/2 cup chicken stock
1/2 cup halved sun-dried tomatoes
1 tbsp. honey
1 medium-hot chili pepper, finely chopped
1/2 tsp. salt
salt and freshly ground black pepper
1/2 cup sour cream
1/2 cup freshly chopped parsley

When dicing the vegetables, cut them as close in size to each other as possible. Place all the ingredients in the slow cooker, except the sour cream and the parsley. Cover and cook on low for 8 hours. Before serving, lightly stir in the sour cream and parsley.

Makes 6 servings

vegetable chili

see variations page 169

On a cold winter's night, nothing beats a steaming bowl of chili, sprinkled with shredded cheddar cheese and with sour cream on the side. Leave out the chili pepper, if you prefer it mild.

1 large onion, coarsely chopped
2 cloves garlic, crushed
2 carrots, chopped
2 zucchini, sliced
2 stalks celery, sliced
1 red bell pepper, seeded and chopped
1 green bell pepper, seeded and chopped
1 (14-oz.) can black beans, drained and rinsed
1 (14-oz.) can chickpeas, drained
1 (14-oz.) can kidney beans, drained and rinsed

1 (14-oz.) can chopped tomatoes in juice
1 (6-oz.) can tomato paste
1 mild or hot green chili, finely chopped
1 tbsp. dried oregano
2 tsp. ground cumin
salt and freshly ground black pepper
2/3 cup freshly chopped cilantro
1 cup shredded cheddar cheese, to serve
2/3 cup sour cream, to serve

Place the vegetables in the slow cooker with the beans, tomatoes, tomato paste, chili, and spices. Cover and cook on low for 6–8 hours. Just before serving, stir in the freshly chopped cilantro. Serve each portion with a sprinkling of shredded cheddar cheese and a good dollop of sour cream.

Makes 6 servings

butternut squash tagine

see variations page 170

Quick and easy to make, this Moroccan-inspired dish is full of goodness while being very low in fat.

1 small butternut squash, peeled,
   seeded, and diced
1 small sweet potato, peeled and diced
1 small red bell pepper, seeded and diced
1 large onion, diced
2 cloves garlic, crushed
1 (14-oz.) can chopped tomatoes in juice

1 (14-oz.) can chickpeas, drained
1 tsp. ground cumin
1 tsp. ground coriander
1 tsp. ground cinnamon
1 tsp. harissa paste (optional)
1/2 cup vegetable stock
2 tbsp. freshly chopped cilantro

Chop the vegetables to roughly the same size. Put all the ingredients, except the cilantro, in the slow cooker. Stir to combine well, cover, and cook on low for 7–8 hours. Just before serving, stir in 2 tablespoons freshly chopped cilantro, and serve with some more cilantro sprinkled on top.

Makes 6 servings

creamy vegetable & cannellini casserole

see variations page 171

This is a delicious meal on its own, but you could also serve it as an accompaniment to grilled meat.

1 tbsp. olive oil
1 large onion, finely chopped
2 cloves garlic, crushed
2 stalks celery, sliced
2 carrots, peeled and chopped
1 small butternut squash, peeled,
    seeded, and chopped
6 ounces baby potatoes
1 cup cauliflower florets

1 (14-oz.) can cannellini beans, drained
1 (14-oz.) can chopped tomatoes in juice
1 tbsp. dried thyme
1 tbsp. paprika
1 tbsp. flour
salt and freshly ground black pepper
3 tbsp. heavy cream
freshly chopped parsley, to serve

In a large skillet, heat the oil and add the onion and garlic. Cook for 5 minutes or until softened. Add the celery and cook for 3 minutes more. Transfer to the slow cooker, and add all the remaining ingredients except the cream and parsley. Cover and cook on low for 6–8 hours. Just before serving, stir in 3 tablespoons heavy cream and sprinkle with freshly chopped parsley.

Makes 4 servings

stuffed bell peppers

see variations page 172

These delicious stuffed peppers are a colorful Mediterranean-style dish, full of great textures and wonderful flavors.

2 red bell peppers
2 green bell peppers
4 shallots, peeled and finely chopped
2 cloves garlic, crushed
2 tomatoes, seeded and chopped

3 cups cooked brown rice
3 tbsp. freshly chopped parsley
1 tsp. chili powder
salt and freshly ground black pepper

Wash and dry the peppers. Carefully slice off the top, leaving the stalks intact if possible, and scoop out the seeds. Reserve the tops. In a medium bowl, mix the shallots, garlic, tomatoes, rice, parsley, and chili powder together. Season with salt and pepper. Spoon mixture into the peppers, add the tops, and stand them upright on a rack in the slow cooker. If you do not have a rack, crunch up some aluminum foil and use that instead. Carefully pour in enough water to come just to the bottom of the peppers, cover, and cook on low for 4–6 hours.

Makes 4 servings

vegetable & cashew biryani

see variations page 173

This aromatic rice dish is excellent on its own, with some Indian-style bread, or served as an accompaniment to the Chicken Dhansak (page 122) or to the Rogan Josh (page 86).

2 tbsp. vegetable oil
2 large onions, finely chopped
2 cloves garlic, crushed
2 tsp. finely chopped and peeled gingerroot
2 tsp. curry powder
1 tsp. garam masala
1 tsp. ground cumin
1 tsp. ground cinnamon
6 green cardamom pods
1 red bell pepper, seeded and diced
1 small sweet potato, peeled and diced

1 cup sliced green beans
1 cup frozen peas
salt and freshly ground black pepper
1 1/4 cups vegetable stock
1/2 cup coconut milk
1 cup roasted salted cashews
3 good pinches saffron
1 tsp. rosewater
3 tbsp. boiling water
3 cups basmati rice, well rinsed and drained
freshly chopped cilantro, to serve

Butter the bottom and sides of the slow cooker pot. In a large skillet, heat the oil and fry the onions and garlic for 5 minutes, or until softened. Add the ginger and cook for another minute. Stir in the curry powder, garam masala, cumin, cinnamon, and cardamom pods, and cook for 4 minutes. Transfer to the slow cooker, and add the red pepper, sweet potato, green beans, and peas. Season with salt and pepper. Pour in vegetable stock and coconut milk, and stir to combine. Scatter the cashews on top. In a small bowl, mix the saffron, rosewater, and boiling water. In a medium saucepan, boil the rice for 5 minutes only, and drain. Spoon the rice onto the vegetables in the slow cooker, and drizzle with the rosewater mixture. Cover and cook on low for 4 hours. Serve sprinkled with cilantro.

Makes 6–8 servings

eggplant parmigiana

see variations page 174

Dairy products do not stand up very well to the long slow cooking associated with slow cookers, but of all the cheeses, Parmesan is one of the most robust.

3 tbsp. olive oil
3 cloves garlic, crushed
2 shallots, peeled and finely chopped
1 tsp. dried oregano
2 (14-oz.) cans chopped tomatoes in juice
2 tbsp. tomato paste
1 tsp. sugar

salt and freshly ground black pepper
3 small firm eggplants, cut into 1/4-inch slices
1/2 cup fresh basil leaves, plus more to garnish
1/2 cup shredded Parmesan cheese
1 cup dry breadcrumbs, to serve

In a large skillet, heat 2 tablespoons olive oil and gently fry the garlic, shallots, and oregano, being careful not to let the oil get too hot or the garlic will be bitter. Cook for 5 minutes. Add the tomatoes and tomato paste, and cook for 10 minutes, stirring continuously. Add the sugar and season with salt and pepper. Place half the tomato sauce in the bottom of the slow cooker, and layer the eggplant slices on top, sprinkling fresh basil and Parmesan cheese between the layers, and staggering the slices to fit the slow cooker. Finish with the rest of the tomato sauce and give the pot a shake to distribute the sauce through the layers. Cover and cook on low for 4 hours. Just before serving, heat the remaining tablespoon olive oil in the skillet, and fry the breadcrumbs until crisp. Serve each portion sprinkled with the breadcrumbs and freshly chopped basil.

Makes 6 servings

mexican chili-bean tortilla lasagna

see variations page 175

This lasagna is made with tortillas instead of pasta, and the cheese is added near the end. If you prefer it less spicy, leave out the fresh chili. If your tortillas are too big, cut them to fit.

2 tbsp. vegetable oil
1 large onion, finely chopped
2 cloves garlic, crushed
1 yellow bell pepper, seeded and chopped
1 cup sliced mushrooms
2 tsp. ground cumin
1 tsp. chili powder
1 tsp. dried oregano
1 fresh green chili, seeded and finely chopped

1 (14-oz.) can chopped tomatoes in juice
1 (14-oz.) can black beans, rinsed and drained
1 (14-oz.) can whole kernel corn, drained
4 tbsp. freshly chopped cilantro
8 small corn tortillas
1 cup sour cream
2 cups shredded cheddar cheese
3 tbsp. freshly chopped cilantro, to serve

In a large skillet, heat the oil and fry the onion and garlic for 5 minutes until softened. Add the pepper and mushrooms and cook for 5 minutes. Add the cumin, chili powder, oregano, and fresh chili, and cook for a further 3 minutes. Add the tomatoes, beans, corn, and cilantro. Layer the tortillas with the sauce in the slow cooker, starting with a layer of tortillas and finishing with a layer of sauce. Cover and cook on low for 5–6 hours. Thirty minutes before the end of the cooking time, mix the sour cream with 1 cup cheddar and spread over the top of the lasagna. Serve sprinkled with cheddar cheese and cilantro.

Makes 6 servings

turkish stuffed eggplant

see base recipe page 153

turkish stuffed eggplant with mozzarella & celery
Prepare the basic recipe, omitting the pine nuts. Add 1/2 cup shredded mozzarella cheese and 1 finely chopped celery stalk before filling the eggplant shells.

turkish stuffed eggplant with lamb
Prepare the basic recipe, omitting the pine nuts. Add 1 cup ground lamb to the skillet with the onion, and cook for 10 minutes until nicely browned. Proceed with the basic recipe.

turkish stuffed eggplant with crab
Prepare the basic recipe, omitting the pine nuts. Add 1 cup prepared fresh or canned crabmeat before filling the eggplant shells.

turkish stuffed eggplant with mixed beans
Prepare the basic recipe, adding 2/3 cup canned mixed beans before filling the eggplant shells.

variations

hungarian vegetable stew

see base recipe page 155

hungarian vegetable stew with mushrooms
Prepare the basic recipe, adding 1 cup sliced mushrooms 2 hours before the end of the cooking time.

hungarian vegetable stew with leeks & apple
Prepare the basic recipe, adding 1 cup sliced leeks and 1 peeled, cored, and chopped tart green apple.

hungarian vegetable stew with cranberries
Prepare the basic recipe, adding 1/2 cup dried cranberries.

hungarian vegetable stew with puy lentils
Prepare the basic recipe, adding 1/2 cup canned puy (French) lentils.

hungarian vegetable stew with cashews
Prepare the basic recipe, adding 1/2 cup unsalted cashews with the sour cream and parsley.

vegetable chili

see base recipe page 156

vegetable chili with corn & cashews
Prepare the basic recipe, adding 1 drained (12-ounce) can whole kernel corn and 1 cup unsalted cashews 30 minutes before the end of the cooking time.

vegetable chili with lentils & pine nuts
Prepare the basic recipe, adding 1 drained (14-ounce) can puy lentils and 1/2 cup pine nuts to the casserole 30 minutes before the end of the cooking time.

vegetable chili with herbed couscous
Prepare the basic recipe, serving the chili with herbed couscous. Add 2 teaspoons dried mixed Italian herbs salt and freshly ground black pepper, and 2 lightly sautéed shallots to plain couscous.

vegetable chili with avocado salsa
Prepare the basic recipe and serve it with avocado salsa, made by removing the skin from 1 avocado and dicing the flesh into a small bowl. Add 1 diced large tomato, 1/2 diced small red onion, 1 tablespoon lime juice, 2 tablespoons freshly chopped cilantro, and 2 teaspoons olive oil. Mix well.

variations

butternut squash tagine

see base recipe page 159

butternut squash & apricot tagine

Prepare the basic recipe, adding 1 cup dried apricots with the vegetables.

butternut squash & spinach tagine

Prepare the basic recipe, adding 2 cups fresh spinach and 1/2 cup pine nuts 30 minutes before the end of the cooking time.

butternut squash tagine with olives & lemon

Prepare the basic recipe, adding 1/3 cup pitted black olives and the grated rind of 1 lemon 30 minutes before the end of the cooking time.

butternut squash tagine with almonds & raisins

Prepare the basic recipe, adding 1/2 cup sliced almonds and 1/2 cup raisins 30 minutes before the end of the cooking time.

butternut squash tagine with chipotle chilies

Prepare the basic recipe, adding 2 finely chopped chipotle chilies 30 minutes before the end of the cooking time.

creamy vegetable & cannellini casserole

see base recipe page 160

creamy vegetable & black-eyed pea casserole with paprika

Prepare the basic recipe, replacing the cannellini beans with black-eyed peas.
Add 2 teaspoons paprika to the onions in the skillet.

creamy vegetable, beet & cannellini casserole

Prepare the basic recipe, adding 2 peeled and diced small beets to the casserole
with the rest of the vegetables.

creamy vegetable, celeriac & cannellini casserole

Prepare the basic recipe, adding 1 celeriac bulb, peeled and diced just before
using, with the rest of the ingredients.

creamy vegetables & cannellini with pasta

Prepare the basic recipe. Add an extra tablespoon of heavy cream and 2 cups
cooked penne pasta to the casserole with the rest of the heavy cream. Let
warm through for an extra 20 minutes before serving.

variations

stuffed bell peppers

see base recipe page 162

stuffed bell peppers with couscous, spinach & pine nuts

Prepare the basic recipe, omitting the rice, parsley, and chili powder. Substitute 3 cups cooked couscous, 1 cup wilted spinach, 1/4 cup pine nuts, and 1 teaspoon ground cumin.

stuffed bell peppers with rice, red onion & sardines

Prepare the basic recipe, omitting the shallots and chili powder. Substitute 1 small red onion, finely chopped and lightly sautéed, and 1 can sardines, bones removed, and flaked.

stuffed bell peppers with rice & mint

Prepare the basic recipe, replacing the chili powder with 2 tablespoons freshly chopped mint and 1 teaspoon ground coriander.

stuffed bell peppers with couscous, zucchini & basil

Prepare the basic recipe, omitting the chili powder and replacing the rice with 3 cups cooked couscous. Add 1 chopped zucchini and 1 cup freshly chopped basil.

variations

vegetable & cashew biryani

see base recipe page 163

vegetable & cashew biryani with potato & golden raisins
Prepare the basic recipe, replacing the sweet potato with a potato. Add 1/2 cup golden raisins with the cashews.

vegetable & cashew biryani with carrots & mint
Prepare the basic recipe, adding 1 cup chopped carrots and 2 tablespoons freshly chopped mint.

vegetable & cashew biryani with tomatoes & chili
Prepare the basic recipe, adding 2 chopped tomatoes and 1 finely chopped red chili.

vegetable & almond biryani with celeriac
Prepare the basic recipe, replacing the sweet potato and cashews with diced celeriac and sliced almonds.

vegetable & cashew biryani with pumpkin & coconut
Prepare the basic recipe, replacing the sweet potato with peeled and chopped pumpkin and adding 1/4 cup flaked unsweetened coconut.

variations

eggplant parmigiana

see base recipe page 165

eggplant parmigiana with red onion & zucchini
Prepare the basic recipe, adding 1 small red onion and 1 small zucchini, both chopped and lightly sautéed, to the layers in the slow cooker.

eggplant parmigiana with bell pepper & pine nuts
Prepare the basic recipe, adding 1 seeded and sliced green bell pepper and 1/2 cup pine nuts to the layers with the eggplant.

eggplant parmigiana with spinach & chili
Prepare the basic recipe, adding 2 cups fresh spinach leaves and 1 finely chopped red chili to the layers with the eggplant.

eggplant parmigiana with sun-dried tomatoes
Prepare the basic recipe, adding 1 cup halved sun-dried tomatoes to the layers with the eggplant.

mexican chili–bean tortilla lasagna

see base recipe page 166

mexican lasagna with pasta
Prepare the basic recipe, omitting the tortillas and substituting cooked lasagna noodles. Shorten the cooking time to 4 hours on low.

mexican lasagna with tequila & fajita seasoning
Prepare the basic recipe, adding 2 tablespoons tequila to the sauce. Replace the spices with 1 tablespoon fajita seasoning.

mexican lasagna with red kidney beans
Prepare the basic recipe, replacing the black beans with red kidney beans.

mexican lasagna with chili, beans, tortillas & guacamole
Prepare the basic recipe, serving with a side of fresh guacamole. Mash together 3 finely chopped mild chilies, 1 finely chopped shallot, 2 finely chopped and seeded tomatoes, and the flesh of 3 ripe avocados. Thin the mixture with 1–2 tablespoons water and the juice of 1/2 lime. Use as soon as possible.

vegetable sides

From spicy potatoes to orange-glazed carrots and caramelized onions, interesting flavors and different textures encourage children and adults alike to eat vegetables. And the ease of cooking them in a slow cooker is an added bonus for the cook.

spicy red cabbage with apple

see variations page 193

This is a traditional dish to serve with roast turkey or pork roast, and is delicious cold as well as hot.

1 red onion, finely chopped
1 clove garlic, crushed
1 medium red cabbage, finely shredded
1 tbsp. brown sugar
1 tbsp. honey

1 tbsp. tomato paste
1 apple, peeled, cored, and finely chopped
1 1/2 tbsp. red wine vinegar
1 cup vegetable stock
salt and freshly ground black pepper, to taste

Place all the ingredients in the slow cooker, cover, and cook on low for 7–8 hours.

Makes 8 servings

orange-glazed carrots

see variations page 194

This is very quick to throw together, and the result is a really interesting and different way of enjoying carrots.

2 lbs. baby carrots
1/2 cup freshly squeezed orange juice
grated rind of 2 oranges
2 tbsp. butter

1/4 cup honey
salt and freshly ground black pepper, to taste
freshly chopped parsley, to serve

Put all the ingredients in the slow cooker, cover, and cook on low for 6–8 hours, or until the carrots are tender. Serve sprinkled with freshly chopped parsley.

Makes 6 servings

braised celery

see variations page 195

Celery is an underrated vegetable, often eaten in a salad, but surprising delicious braised in vegetable stock with onions and garlic.

2 1/2 lbs. celery
2 tbsp. olive oil
2 cloves garlic, crushed
1 large onion, finely chopped
1–2 tsp. dried red pepper flakes

1 cup vegetable stock
2 tbsp. tomato paste
salt and freshly ground black pepper
freshly chopped parsley, to serve

Clean the celery thoroughly, cut off the leaves, and remove the strings from the outer stalks. Cut into 4-inch lengths. In a large skillet, heat the olive oil and cook the onion and garlic until softened, about 5 minutes. Transfer to the slow cooker, and add the celery. In a medium saucepan, add the tomato paste to the vegetable stock, and heat until the tomato paste has dissolved into the liquid. Add to the slow cooker with the red pepper flakes, season with salt and pepper, cover, and cook on low for 2–3 hours. Serve sprinkled with chopped parsley.

Makes 6 servings

caramelized onions

see variations page 196

These onions make an interesting side dish, as well as a flavorful addition to gravy, soups, stews, and casseroles. Keep some in the refrigerator to use when needed.

5 lbs. onions, sliced
1/2 cup butter
2 tsp. sugar

1 tbsp. balsamic vinegar
pinch of salt

Place the onions in the slow cooker with the butter, sugar, balsamic vinegar, and salt. Cook on high for 1-3 hours, uncovered. Give a stir, cover, turn the heat down to low, and cook for 8-10 hours. If possible, give a stir occasionally. The onions will slowly caramelize as the liquid gently evaporates, and they will gradually become a silky brown color. Store in a plastic container and keep in the refrigerator for up to a month.

Makes about 1 1/2 lbs

bombay potatoes

see variations page 197

These mildly spiced potatoes are a very popular side dish for any Indian meal. Fresh tomatoes are best, but if you wish, you can use canned tomatoes.

1 tbsp. olive oil
1 large onion, finely chopped
2 cloves garlic, crushed
2 stalks celery, sliced
2 carrots, peeled and chopped
1 small butternut squash, peeled,
    seeded, and chopped
6 oz. baby potatoes
1 cup cauliflower florets

1 (14-oz.) can cannellini beans, drained
1 (14-oz.) can chopped tomatoes in juice
1 tbsp. dried thyme
1 tbsp. paprika
1 tbsp. flour
salt and freshly ground black pepper
3 tbsp. heavy cream
freshly chopped parsley, to serve

Grease the base and sides of the pot in the slow cooker with butter. In a large skillet, heat the oil and fry the mustard seeds until they start to pop. Add the chili powder, turmeric, cumin, garam masala, and ginger, and cook for 3 minutes. Add the potatoes and turn them around in the oil and spices, then transfer to the slow cooker. Add the tomatoes, salt and pepper, and half the cilantro. Stir to mix it all together, cover, and cook on low for 6–8 hours.

Before serving, stir in the remaining cilantro.

Makes 6 servings

ratatouille with oregano & basil

see variations page 198

This is slightly different from the ratatouille in chapter 4. If you wish, you can cook the onion and garlic in a skillet for 5 minutes, until softened, instead of heating in the slow cooker.

1 tbsp. olive oil
1 large red onion, coarsely chopped
2 cloves garlic, crushed
1 large eggplant, diced
2 large zucchini, diced
1 orange or yellow bell pepper,
    seeded, and diced

2 (14-oz.) cans tomatoes in juice
1 tbsp. tomato paste
2 tsp. dried oregano
1/2 cup fresh basil leaves
salt and freshly ground black pepper

Heat the slow cooker on high for 10 minutes, add the olive oil, onion, and garlic, and leave for 15 minutes, uncovered, stirring occasionally. Turn the heat to low, add the rest of the ingredients, cover, and cook for 6–7 hours.

Makes 6 servings

baked beans

see variations page 199

Very popular all around the world, homemade baked beans are far superior to the canned variety, and you can design them to your own particular preference.

2 cups dried navy beans, sorted, rinsed, and
    soaked overnight
1 large onion, finely chopped
1 2/3 cups canned tomato sauce
4 tbsp. tomato paste
1 tbsp. Worcestershire sauce
1/2 cup ketchup
1 1/2 cups vegetable stock or water

1/3 cup molasses
1/2 cup brown sugar
2 tbsp. red wine vinegar
1 tbsp. Dijon mustard
2 tsp. cayenne pepper
2 tsp. paprika
salt and freshly ground black pepper

Drain the beans, place them in a saucepan, cover with water, and bring to a boil. Lower the heat and simmer for 15 minutes, then drain. Place the beans, onion, tomato sauce, tomato paste, Worcestershire sauce, ketchup, stock, molasses, brown sugar, and vinegar in the slow cooker. Cook on low for 8–10 hours, or until the beans are tender.

One hour before the end of the cooking time, add the mustard, cayenne pepper, paprika, and salt and pepper to taste.

Makes 8 servings

scalloped potatoes boulangères

see variations page 200

Potatoes take a very long time to cook in the slow cooker, so slice them as thinly as possible, using a mandoline if you have one.

2 tbsp. olive oil

2–3 onions, finely sliced

2 cloves garlic, crushed

4–6 potatoes, peeled and very thinly sliced

salt and freshly ground black pepper

1/2 cup freshly chopped parsley

1 1/4 cups vegetable or chicken stock

In a large skillet, heat the oil and cook the onions and garlic for 5 minutes, or until softened and just starting to color. Grease the pot in the slow cooker with butter and start filling it, starting with a thin layer of onion, then potatoes, salt, pepper, and parsley. Repeat until you have used up all the potatoes and onions. Add the stock slowly, cover, and cook on low for 8–9 hours.

Makes 6 servings

sweet potato casserole with coconut & pecans

see variations page 201

Sweet potato casserole is a traditional Thanksgiving dish, and when your oven is filled with a turkey, it's great to use the slow cooker to cook this dish. The spices give it a real fall aroma and the sweetness of the potatoes means the kids will love it.

4–5 large sweet potatoes (to make about
   4 cups mashed)
1/3 cup butter, melted
1/2 cup granulated sugar
3 tbsp. light brown sugar
2 large eggs, lightly beaten
1 tsp. vanilla extract
1 tsp. ground cinnamon

1/2 tsp. ground nutmeg
1/3 cup heavy cream
for the topping
3/4 cup chopped pecans
1/2 cup flaked coconut
3/4 cup light brown sugar
1/4 cup flour
2 tbsp. butter, melted

Peel the potatoes, cut into chunks, and place in a large saucepan. Cover with water and bring to a boil. Reduce the heat slightly and simmer for 20–25 minutes, or until tender. Drain and mash thoroughly, and cool slightly. In a large bowl, combine the potatoes, butter, granulated sugar, brown sugar, eggs, vanilla, and spices, and beat until smooth. Add the cream, stir, and transfer to the slow cooker. In a small bowl, combine the pecans, coconut, brown sugar, flour, and melted butter. Sprinkle over the potatoes. Cover and cook on low for 3–4 hours.

Makes 8 servings

variations

spicy red cabbage with apple

see base recipe page 177

spicy red cabbage with apple & raisins
Prepare the basic recipe, adding 1/2 cup raisins.

spicy red & green cabbage with apple & walnuts
Prepare the basic recipe, replacing half the red cabbage with green cabbage, and adding 1/2 cup chopped walnuts to the slow cooker 5 minutes before the end of cooking time.

spicy red cabbage with apple & currant jelly
Prepare the basic recipe, adding 2 tablespoons currant jelly.

spicy red cabbage with apple & orange
Prepare the basic recipe, adding the grated rind of 1 orange.

spicy red cabbage with apple & prunes
Prepare the basic recipe, adding 1 cup pitted canned prunes.

variations

orange glazed carrots

see base recipe page 179

pineapple- & coconut-glazed carrots

Prepare the basic recipe, omitting the orange juice and rind, and substituting 1 (8-ounce) can crushed pineapple with juice. Serve sprinkled with shredded coconut.

balsamic-glazed carrots

Prepare the basic recipe, omitting the orange juice and rind, and substituting vegetable stock and 2 tablespoon balsamic vinegar.

orange-glazed carrots with cilantro

Prepare the basic recipe, stirring 1/2 cup freshly chopped cilantro into the carrots just before the end of cooking time.

orange- & maple-glazed parsnips

Prepare the basic recipe, replacing the carrots with peeled and chopped parsnips, and adding 2 tablespoons maple syrup and 1 teaspoon ground cinnamon.

lemon-glazed carrots

Prepare the basic recipe, omitting the orange juice and rind, and substituting lemon juice and lemon rind.

braised celery

see base recipe page 180

braised celery with carrots & cilantro
Prepare the basic recipe, adding 2 peeled and diced carrots to the celery in the slow cooker. Substitute freshly chopped cilantro for the parsley.

braised celery with white wine
Prepare the basic recipe, replacing the vegetable stock with dry white wine.

braised celery with olives
Prepare the basic recipe, adding 1/2 cup pitted black olives to the slow cooker with the celery.

braised celery & artichokes
Prepare the basic recipe, replacing half the celery with canned artichokes.

braised celery with bacon
Prepare the basic recipe, adding 1/2 cup chopped bacon to the skillet with the onion and garlic.

variations

caramelized onions

see base recipe page 183

caramelized onions with pine nuts
Prepare the basic recipe, and serve with 1 tablespoon pine nuts sprinkled on each portion.

caramelized onions with mushrooms
Prepare the basic recipe. Remove onions from the refrigerator, and place in a medium saucepan. Add 1/4 cup sliced mushrooms per serving, and cook over medium heat until the mushrooms are softened.

caramelized onion quiche
Prepare the basic recipe. When the onions have cooled, place 4 tablespoons onions in the bottom of a pastry-lined pie pan. In a medium bowl, mix together 2 large eggs, 2 large egg yolks, and 1 cup half-and-half. Add to the onions and bake at 375°F for about 25–30 minutes, until filling is set and pastry is golden.

caramelized onion omelet
Prepare the basic recipe. Make an omelet with 2 beaten eggs, fried in a small skillet with 1 teaspoon vegetable oil. Add 2 tablespoons caramelized onions, cook for a minute or two, then carefully flip. Makes 1 serving.

variations

bombay potatoes

see base recipe page 184

bombay potatoes with peppers & rosemary
Prepare the basic recipe, adding 1 seeded and chopped green bell pepper
and 2 teaspoons dried rosemary to the slow cooker.

bombay potatoes with cardamom & poppy seeds
Prepare the basic recipe, adding 6 cardamom seeds and 2 teaspoons poppy
seeds to the slow cooker.

bombay potatoes with cashews & star anise
Prepare the basic recipe, adding 1/4 cup cashew nuts and 3 star anise to the
slow cooker. Remove the star anise, if possible, before serving.

bombay potatoes with onions & apples
Prepare the basic recipe, adding 1 finely chopped small onion to the skillet
after the mustard seeds, and 1 peeled and finely chopped small apple to the
slow cooker.

bombay potatoes with spinach & pine nuts
Prepare the basic recipe, adding 2 cups chopped fresh spinach leaves and
1/4 cup pine nuts to the slow cooker.

variations

ratatouille with oregano & basil

see base recipe page 187

spicy ratatouille with oregano & basil
Prepare the basic recipe, adding 2 teaspoons chili powder and 2 finely chopped mild green chilies.

ratatouille pasta sauce
Prepare the basic recipe. To serve, blend some ratatouille with an immersion blender until slightly mashed, and serve over pasta.

baked ratatouille with cheese
Prepare the basic recipe. Then place the ratatouille in an ovenproof dish, and pour on cheese sauce, sprinkle with shredded cheddar cheese, and broil to brown the cheese. Make the cheese sauce by melting 2 tablespoons butter in a saucepan, stir in 2 tablespoons flour, and cook for 2 minutes. Gradually stir in 1 cup milk, and bring just to a simmer. Stir in 1/2 cup shredded cheddar cheese, 1 teaspoon Dijon mustard, and salt and freshly ground black pepper.

ratatouille with cilantro & sun-dried tomatoes
Prepare the basic recipe, omitting the basil. Substitute freshly chopped cilantro, adding half at the beginning and half at the end. Add 1/2 cup sun-dried tomatoes to the slow cooker.

variations

baked beans

see base recipe page 189

baked beans with bourbon & chorizo
Prepare the basic recipe, replacing the red wine vinegar with bourbon. Add
1 cup chopped chorizo to the slow cooker with the beans.

baked beans with maple syrup & apple
Prepare the basic recipe, replacing the red wine vinegar with maple syrup.
Add 2 eating apples, peeled, cored, and finely chopped to the slow cooker
with the beans.

baked beans with bacon
Prepare the basic recipe, adding 1 cup chopped bacon, cooked until crisp, to
the slow cooker with the beans.

baked beans with hot dogs
Prepare the basic recipe, adding 2 packs hot dogs, sliced, to the slow cooker
with the beans.

baked beans with bourbon & pineapple
Prepare the basic recipe, adding 1 well-drained (15-ounce) can crushed
pineapple, 1/3 cup strong coffee, 1/2 cup bourbon, and 1/2 cup bottled
chili sauce to the slow cooker with the beans.

variations

scalloped potatoes boulangère

see base recipe page 190

scalloped potatoes boulangère with rosemary
Prepare the basic recipe, adding 2 tablespoons fresh rosemary, chopped and bruised in a mortar and pestle, at the same time as the parsley in the layers.

scalloped potatoes & leeks boulangère
Prepare the basic recipe, replacing the onions and garlic with 4 leeks, thinly sliced and lightly sautéed.

scalloped white & sweet potatoes boulangère
Prepare the basic recipe, replacing 1 potato with 1 sweet potato. Add 2 tablespoons fresh rosemary, chopped and bruised in a mortar and pestle, at the same time as the parsley.

scalloped potatoes boulangère with sage
Prepare the basic recipe, adding 3 tablespoons chopped fresh sage at the same time as the parsley.

scalloped potatoes & apple boulangère
Prepare the basic recipe, replacing the stock with apple cider. Add 1 dessert apple, peeled, cored, and very finely chopped, to the layers with the parsley.

sweet potato casserole with coconut & pecans

see base recipe page 192

sweet potato casserole with marshmallows & pecans
Prepare the basic recipe, omitting the topping, and substituting mini marshmallows.

sweet potato & squash casserole
Prepare the basic recipe, omitting the topping. Replace half the sweet potatoes with 2 cups peeled and chopped butternut squash. Omit both sugars and vanilla extract and use 1 cup lightly sautéed chopped onion and 2 teaspoons dried rosemary.

sweet potato casserole with orange & pecans
Prepare the basic recipe, omitting the vanilla extract and substituting the juice and grated rind of 1 large orange.

sweet potato, carrot & rutabaga casserole
Prepare the basic recipe, omitting the topping. Replace half the sweet potatoes with a mixture of peeled and chopped carrots and rutabaga. Omit both sugars, vanilla extract, and cinnamon.

sweet potato casserole with green onion, parsley & pine nuts
Prepare the basic recipe, omitting the granulated sugar, vanilla, and cinnamon and adding 1 cup chopped green onions and 1/2 cup freshly chopped parsley. Replace the topping with 1 cup pine nuts.

grains, lentils & beans

For vegetarians and meat-eaters alike, grains, lentils, and beans are a good source not only of protein and vitamins, but of fiber too. A slow-cooked, flavorful stew brimming with beans will be irresistible to all the family.

bulgur wheat with red bell pepper

see variations page 218

Long cooking can remove color from vegetables. If you like, you can sauté the onion and red pepper in a little oil, and add them 10 minutes before the end of the cooking time. This dish takes just 5 minutes to prepare.

2 cups bulgur wheat
1 large onion, finely chopped
2 cups sliced mushrooms
1 red bell pepper, seeded and diced
5 cups vegetable stock

2 tbsp. olive oil
2 tsp. dried thyme
2 tsp. soy sauce
salt and freshly ground black pepper to taste
1/2 cup freshly chopped cilantro

Place all the ingredients, except the cilantro, in the slow cooker. Cover and cook on low for 3–3 1/2 hours. Just before serving, stir in the cilantro.

Makes 6 servings

millet & red onion stew

see variations page 219

We can all benefit from adding more whole grains to our diets—they are so good for our digestive system. Millet has a similar consistency and taste to couscous. Although this is called a stew, it does not have a lot of liquid. If you use sodium-free vegetable stock, you'll probably want to add some salt, as whole grains taste very bland and flat without seasoning.

1 cup millet
2 medium red onions, coarsely chopped
2 potatoes, peeled and diced
2 carrots, diced
2 stalks celery, sliced

2 cups sliced mushrooms
3 1/2 cups vegetable stock
1 tsp. dried marjoram
salt and freshly ground black pepper, to taste
1/2 cup freshly chopped parsley

In a large skillet, over medium heat, dry-fry the millet for 5–8 minutes, stirring continuously. Place millet in the slow cooker, add the rest of the ingredients except the parsley, stir, cover, and cook on low for 3–3 1/2 hours. Just before serving, check the seasoning, add parsley, and stir it through.

Makes 4 servings

creamy risotto with spinach

see variations page 220

When risotto is cooked on the stovetop, it requires a lot of stirring, so many people don't want to make it. When it's made in the slow cooker, however, it needs no attention at all.

2 tbsp. olive oil
3 shallots, finely chopped
1 1/4 cups Arborio (risotto) rice
1 cup dry white wine

3 cups chicken stock
freshly ground black pepper
3 cups baby fresh spinach leaves, washed
shredded Parmesan cheese, to serve

Heat the oil in a small saucepan, add the shallots, and cook over medium heat for 5 minutes until softened. Transfer to the slow cooker, add the rice, and turn it around in the shallots and oil until well coated. Add the wine and stock, and season with black pepper. Cook on high for 3–4 hours. Fifteen minutes before the end of the cooking time, add the spinach leaves and mix them in. Serve sprinkled with the shredded Parmesan cheese.

Makes 4 servings

basmati rice pilaf

see variations page 221

This is an amazingly versatile rice dish, to which you can add anything you want. It can be enjoyed on its own or with grilled fish or meat. Adding the peas at the end keeps their color bright.

1 tbsp. olive oil
1 large onion, finely chopped
2 cups basmati rice
4 cups vegetable stock
1 cup finely chopped carrots

salt and freshly ground black pepper
1/2 cup finely chopped red bell pepper
1/2 cup frozen peas, thawed
1/2 cup slivered almonds, toasted
freshly chopped parsley, to serve

Grease the bottom and sides of the pot in the slow cooker with butter. In a large skillet, heat the vegetable oil and fry the onion for 5 minutes until softened. Add the rice, and turn it around to coat it with the oil. Add the stock and bring to a boil. Simmer for 4 minutes only. Transfer rice to the slow cooker, add the carrots, cover, and cook on low for 3 hours.

Thirty minutes before the end of the cooking time, season to taste with salt and pepper, add the red pepper, peas, and slivered almonds. Serve sprinkled with freshly chopped parsley.

Makes 8 servings

mixed grain pilaf

see variations page 222

This pilaf uses a combination of mixed whole grains, which, when eaten as part of a healthy diet, can help reduce the risk of heart disease. Adding vegetables and spices will add flavor.

2 tbsp. sesame oil
1 medium onion, finely chopped
2 cloves garlic, crushed
2 tsp. coriander seeds, crushed
2 tsp. mustard seeds
1 tsp. dried red pepper flakes
1/2 cup quinoa, rinsed
1/2 cup spelt grain, rinsed
1/2 cup bulgur wheat
1/ 2 cup brown lentils, rinsed and picked over

1 cup fresh or frozen fava or lima beans
1 leek, sliced
2 cups sliced mushrooms
1/2 red bell pepper, seeded and diced
5 cups vegetable or chicken stock
salt and freshly ground black pepper
1/4 cup freshly chopped parsley
1/4 cup freshly chopped cilantro
1/4 cup chopped toasted pecans

In a large skillet, heat the oil, add the coriander seeds and mustard seeds, and cook for a minute or two, until the mustard seeds start to jump. Add the onion and garlic and cook for about 5 minutes, or until softened. Transfer to the slow cooker, add the quinoa, spelt, bulgur wheat, lentils, beans, leek, mushrooms, red pepper, and stock. Season with salt and pepper, cover, and cook on low for 4–6 hours.

Just before serving, taste, and adjust the seasoning as needed. Stir in the parsley, cilantro, and pecans.

Makes 6 servings

indian dahl

see variations page 223

You can serve this Indian-spiced thick soup as an appetizer, like a soup, with chapatis, or as part of an Indian-themed meal, with naan bread and Chicken Dhansak (see recipe page 122). Dahl is known for its gorgeous yellow color.

2 tablespoons vegetable oil
1 tbsp. yellow curry powder
1 tbsp. ground turmeric
1 tbsp. paprika
1 tbsp. ground cumin
1 tsp. chili powder
1 tsp. peeled and finely chopped gingerroot

4 cloves garlic, crushed
2 cups dried red lentils, rinsed and picked over
7 cups vegetable stock
2 chicken stock cubes
1 medium potato, peeled and diced small
salt and freshly ground black pepper
freshly chopped cilantro, to serve

In a small saucepan, heat the oil, and gently cook the curry powder, turmeric, paprika, cumin, chili powder, ginger, and garlic for a few minutes to release all the lovely aromas. Transfer to the slow cooker, add the rest of the ingredients, cover, and cook on low for 6–7 hours. Just before serving, check the seasoning and adjust if necessary. Serve sprinkled with freshly chopped cilantro.

Makes 6 servings

garlic chickpeas & lentils

see variations page 224

This aromatic chickpea stew is filling enough to satisfy even the hungriest member of the family.

2 cups dried chickpeas, sorted and soaked
    overnight
2 tbsp. vegetable oil
1 large onion, finely chopped
4 cloves garlic
3 tsp. dried rosemary

1 tsp. tamarind paste
1/2 cup dried red lentils, rinsed and picked over
4 cups vegetable stock
1/2 butternut squash, peeled and diced
1 bay leaf
fresh rosemary, to serve

Drain the chickpeas, place them in a medium saucepan, cover with water, and bring to a boil. Turn the heat down, and simmer for 15 minutes. Drain and transfer to the slow cooker. In a large skillet, heat the vegetable oil, and cook the onion and garlic for 5 minutes, or until softened. Transfer to the slow cooker, and add the rest of the ingredients except the cheese. Cover and cook on low for 7–8 hours.

Just before the end of the cooking time, adjust the seasoning if necessary. Serve sprinkled with fresh rosemary.

Makes 6 servings

lentil, bean & barley casserole

see variations page 225

This casserole is a very hearty and filling dish, one that will satisfy even hardened meat eaters.

1 tbsp. butter
1 tbsp. vegetable oil
1 medium onion, finely chopped
2 cloves garlic, crushed
2 1/2 cups sliced mushrooms
3 1/2 cups vegetable stock
3/4 cup uncooked pearl barley

3/4 cup dried red lentils, rinsed and picked over
2 tsp. dried sage
2 tsp. dried basil
1 cup frozen lima beans
salt and freshly ground black pepper
freshly chopped parsley, to serve

In a small skillet, melt the butter and oil together. Add the onion and garlic and cook for 5 minutes, or until softened. Transfer to the slow cooker and add the other ingredients, except the lima beans and parsley. Cover and cook on low for 10–12 hours. Thirty minutes before the end of the cooking time, stir in the lima beans, and taste, adjusting the seasoning if necessary.

Serve sprinkled with parsley.

Makes 6 servings

mung bean & potato casserole

see variations page 226

Mung beans have a rich and creamy texture. They are an unusual, interesting, and delicious choice for a casserole.

2 cups mung beans, sorted, rinsed, and soaked
   overnight
2 tbsp. vegetable oil
1 large onion, finely chopped
2 cloves garlic, crushed
4 medium potatoes, peeled and diced

2 tsp. dried marjoram
2 large carrots, peeled and diced
2 celery stalks, sliced
2 cups sliced mushrooms
6 cups vegetable stock
salt and freshly ground black pepper, to taste

Drain the mung beans, place them in a medium saucepan, cover with water, and bring to a boil. Turn the heat down and simmer for 15 minutes. Drain and transfer to the slow cooker. In a large skillet, heat the oil and cook the onion and garlic for 5 minutes, or until softened. Transfer to the slow cooker, add the rest of the ingredients, and stir to combine. Cover and cook on low for 10 hours. Just before serving, adjust the seasoning if necessary.

Makes 6 servings

black-eyed peas with bacon

see variations page 227

Black-eyed peas are associated with good luck, and are often eaten at New Year's celebrations. In the Deep South, black-eyed peas are cooked with salt pork in a dish known as Hoppin' John. This version is spicier and very tasty.

1 cup dried black-eyed peas, sorted, rinsed, and
    soaked overnight
1/2 lb. bacon, chopped
1 large onion, finely chopped
2 cloves garlic, crushed
2 tsp. dried oregano
2 tsp. paprika
2 tsp. chili powder (or to taste)
1 tsp. cumin seeds, crushed

1 tsp. coriander seeds, crushed
4 cups Swiss chard or collard greens, washed,
    trimmed, and chopped
1 (14-oz.) can chopped tomatoes in juice
salt and freshly ground black pepper
2 cups frozen whole kernel corn
1 cup basmati or long-grain rice, uncooked

Drain the black-eyed peas and put them in a large saucepan. Cover with water and bring to a boil. Lower the heat and simmer for 1 hour. Drain and set aside. In a large skillet, dry-fry the bacon until browned and crispy. Remove and drain on paper towels. Drain off most of the fat from the skillet, add the onion and garlic, and cook for 5 minutes, or until softened. Add the oregano, paprika, chili powder, cumin, and coriander seeds, and cook for 2 minutes. Transfer to the slow cooker. Add the bacon, the black-eyed peas, the Swiss chard or greens, tomatoes, and salt and pepper. Cook on low for 9–10 hours, or high for 5–6 hours. Add the corn and rice, and cook for another hour on low. Before serving, adjust the seasoning as needed.

Makes 6 servings

variations

bulgur wheat with red bell pepper

see base recipe page 203

bulgur wheat chili
Prepare the basic recipe, replacing the vegetable stock with tomato juice.
Add 1 teaspoon chili powder, 2 finely chopped red chilies, 1 beef stock cube,
1 drained and rinsed (14-ounce can) red kidney beans, and 1 drained and
rinsed (14-ounce can) black beans.

bulgur wheat with red bell pepper, fruit & nuts
Prepare the basic recipe, adding 1/4 cup golden raisins and 1/2 cup cashews
15 minutes before the end of the cooking time.

bulgur wheat with red bell pepper, lemon & olives
Prepare the basic recipe, adding the grated zest of 2 lemons and 1/4 cup
pitted black olives 15 minutes before the end of the cooking time.

bulgur wheat with red bell pepper, spinach & pine nuts
Prepare the basic recipe, adding 1 cup fresh spinach leaves and 1/2 cup pine
nuts 30 minutes before the end of the cooking time.

variations

millet & red onion stew

see base recipe page 205

millet & red onion stew with bacon
Prepare the basic recipe. Just before serving, stir in 1/2 cup chopped bacon, cooked until crispy, with the parsley.

millet & red onion stew with corn & coriander
Prepare the basic recipe, omitting the marjoram, and adding 1 teaspoon ground coriander and 1 teaspoon ground cumin with the rest of the ingredients. Thirty minutes before the end of the cooking time, stir in 1 (12-ounce can) whole kernel corn.

millet & red onion stew with red bell pepper & basil
Prepare the basic recipe, omitting the marjoram. Fifteen minutes before the end of the cooking time, add 1 red bell pepper, seeded, chopped, and sautéed for 5 minutes in a little oil, and 1 cup fresh basil leaves to the slow cooker.

millet & red onion stew with tomatoes
Prepare the basic recipe, adding 2 seeded and chopped tomatoes and 1 cup fresh basil leaves 15 minutes before the end of the cooking time.

variations

creamy risotto with spinach

see base recipe page 206

creamy risotto with watercress & peas

Prepare the basic recipe, omitting the spinach. Add 1 cup frozen peas
30 minutes before the end of the cooking time and 1 cup roughly
chopped watercress 10 minutes later.

creamy risotto with pine nuts & basil

Prepare the basic recipe, omitting the spinach. Add 1/2 cup pine nuts and
2 tablespoons freshly chopped basil 10 minutes before the end of cooking time.

creamy risotto with butternut squash & sage

Prepare the basic recipe, omitting the spinach. Add 2/3 cup chopped butternut
squash at the same time as the rice, and add 2 tablespoons freshly chopped
sage 10 minutes before the end of the cooking time.

creamy risotto with asparagus, lemon & mint

Prepare the basic recipe, omitting the spinach. Thirty minutes before the end
of the cooking time, add 6–8 sliced asparagus spears, and 20 minutes later, add
1 teaspoon finely grated lemon zest and 1 tablespoon freshly chopped mint.

basmati rice pilaf

see base recipe page 207

spicy basmati rice pilaf with fruit & nuts
Prepare the basic recipe, adding 1 teaspoon ground cumin, 1 teaspoon
ground coriander, and 2 crushed cloves garlic to the skillet with the onion.
Add 1/4 cup raisins, 1/4 cup chopped dried apricots, and 1/4 cup cashew
nuts to the slow cooker with the peas.

basmati rice pilaf with celery & broccoli
Prepare the basic recipe, adding 1/4 cup cooked and chopped celery and
1/2 cup cooked broccoli florets to the slow cooker with the red pepper
and peas.

basmati rice pilaf with butternut squash
Prepare the basic recipe, adding 1/2 cup peeled and diced butternut squash
to the slow cooker with the carrots.

basmati rice pilaf with mushrooms & sun-dried tomatoes
Prepare the basic recipe, omitting the carrots and peas. Add 1 cup sliced
mushrooms with the stock and onions, and 1/4 cup sun-dried tomatoes
with the red bell pepper.

variations

mixed grain pilaf

see base recipe page 208

mixed grain pilaf with swiss chard
Prepare the basic recipe, adding 2 cups washed and chopped Swiss chard and substituting walnuts for the pecans.

mixed grain pilaf with broccoli
Prepare the basic recipe, adding 2 cups broccoli florets and substituting toasted pistachio nuts for the pecans.

mixed grain pilaf with mint & green onions
Prepare the basic recipe, adding 1/4 cup freshly chopped mint and 1 cup chopped green onions with the parsley and cilantro.

mixed grain pilaf with apricots & almonds
Prepare the basic recipe, adding 1/3 cup chopped dried apricots to the slow cooker with the parsley and cilantro, and substituting chopped toasted almonds for the pecans.

mixed grain pilaf with peas
Prepare the basic recipe, adding 1 cup fresh or frozen peas 1 hour before the end of the cooking time.

indian dahl

see base recipe page 211

indian dahl with fennel & raisins
Prepare the basic recipe, adding 1 teaspoon fennel seeds to the saucepan
with the rest of the spices. Add 1/4 cup raisins to the slow cooker just
before serving.

indian dahl with red bell pepper & coconut milk
Prepare the basic recipe, replacing 1 cup stock with coconut milk and adding
1 seeded and chopped red bell pepper.

indian dahl with eggplant
Prepare the basic recipe, adding 1 diced medium eggplant.

indian dahl with apple & celery
Prepare the basic recipe, adding 1 peeled, cored, and diced apple and 2 diced
celery stalks.

indian dahl with tomatoes & yogurt
Prepare the basic recipe, replacing 2 cups vegetable stock with 2 cups
canned tomatoes in juice. Serve with a generous dollop of plain yogurt.

variations

garlic chickpeas & lentils

see base recipe page 212

garlic chickpeas & lentils with spices
Prepare the basic recipe, omitting the rosemary. Add 1 teaspoon each of
turmeric, paprika, garam masala, ground ginger, and curry powder to the skillet
with the onion. Omit the cheddar cheese and stir in 1 cup crumbled feta
cheese and 1/4 cup freshly chopped parsley, just before serving.

garlic chickpeas & lentils with olives & tomatoes
Prepare the basic recipe, adding 2/3 cup pitted green olives and 4 seeded and
chopped tomatoes just before serving.

garlic chickpeas & lentils with lemon & thyme
Prepare the basic recipe, adding 2 teaspoons dried thyme. Just before serving,
add the juice and grated rind of 1 lemon and 1/4 cup freshly chopped parsley.

garlic chickpeas & lentils with tomatoes & pine nuts
Prepare the basic recipe, adding 4 seeded and chopped tomatoes and 1/2 cup
pine nuts to the slow cooker just before the end of the cooking time.

lentil, bean & barley casserole

see base recipe page 214

lentil, red kidney bean & barley casserole
Prepare the basic recipe, replacing the lima beans with 1 (16-ounce) can red kidney beans, drained and rinsed. Add 1 finely chopped mild green chili just before serving. Instead of parsley, sprinkle with freshly chopped cilantro.

lentil, bean & barley casserole with butternut squash
Prepare the basic recipe, adding 1/2 butternut squash, peeled, seeded, and diced, to the slow cooker with the rest of the ingredients.

lentil, bean & barley casserole with chorizo
Prepare the basic recipe, adding 1 cup chopped chorizo to the slow cooker 1 hour before the end of the cooking time. Serve sprinkled with shredded cheddar cheese.

lentil, bean & barley casserole with tofu
Prepare the basic recipe, adding 1 cup chopped tofu to the slow cooker 1 hour before the end of the cooking time.

variations

mung bean & potato casserole

see base recipe page 215

mung bean & potato casserole with tamarind
Prepare the basic recipe, adding 2 teaspoons tamarind paste with the rest of the ingredients.

mung bean & sweet potato casserole
Prepare the basic recipe, replacing the potatoes with sweet potatoes. Add 1/2 cup cashew nuts just before serving.

mung bean, potato & celeriac casserole
Prepare the basic recipe, omitting the marjoram. Add 1 cup peeled and diced celeriac with the mung beans, and add 1/2 cup fresh basil leaves, just before serving.

mung bean, butter bean & potato casserole
Prepare the basic recipe, adding 1 drained (14-ounce) can butter beans 30 minutes before the end of the cooking time.

variations

black-eyed peas with bacon

see base recipe page 216

black-eyed peas with ham hock
Prepare the basic recipe, omitting the bacon. Substitute a smoked ham hock, added to the slow cooker with the vegetables. Just before serving, remove the meat from the bone and return the meat to the slow cooker.

black-eyed peas with mushrooms
Prepare the basic recipe, adding 2 cups sliced mushrooms to the slow cooker with the rest of the vegetables.

black-eyed peas with red bell pepper & cilantro
Prepare the basic recipe, adding 1 seeded and chopped red bell pepper to the slow cooker with the rest of the vegetables. Stir in 1/3 cup freshly chopped cilantro just before serving.

black-eyed peas with butternut squash
Prepare the basic recipe, adding 1/2 butternut squash, peeled and diced, to the slow cooker with the rest of the ingredients.

fruits &
desserts

Steamed puddings will always be an obvious choice

for your slow cooker, but other desserts, fruit

cobblers, cakes, and even brownies are delicious

when made in a slow cooker.

sticky toffee pudding

see variations page 248

Serve with ice cream, whipped cream, or custard.

for the sauce
1/2 cup butter
1 tbsp. light corn syrup
3/4 cup light brown sugar
2 tbsp. heavy cream
1 tsp. vanilla extract
for the pudding
7 oz. dates, pitted and chopped

1 cup water
1 tsp. baking soda
1 1/4 cups butter, softened, plus
    extra for greasing
1 cup dark brown sugar
2 eggs
1 1/2 cups self-rising flour
1/2 tsp. ground ginger

First make the sauce. Melt the butter in a small saucepan over low heat. Add the sugar and the corn syrup, stirring constantly. Bring to a boil, then simmer for 5 minutes. Remove from the heat. When cool, add the cream and vanilla, and stir. Set aside. Next, make the pudding. Put the dates into a saucepan, add the water, and bring to a boil. Add the baking soda and stir. Simmer for 5 minutes, remove from the heat, and let cool. In a large bowl, place the softened butter, brown sugar, eggs, flour, and gingerroot. Whisk until just blended. Add the cooled dates and mix again until just blended. Put 3 tablespoons of the sauce in a 2-quart baking dish, and pour in the pudding mixture. Cover with a layer of waxed paper and a layer of foil, both pleated to allow room for expansion. Tie with string, making a handle to use to lift the pudding out of the slow cooker. Place a layer of crumpled foil in the bottom of the slow cooker, put the baking dish on top, and pour in enough water to come just under halfway up the side of the dish. Cook on high for 4 hours, or on low for 8–9 hours. Just before serving, heat the sauce, and serve the pudding warm with the sauce poured on top.
Makes 6–8 servings

carrot cake with orange icing

see variations page 249

One would not normally think of making cakes in the slow cooker, but try it. You will be amazed at how moist and light they are. The icing, made with orange juice, contrasts beautifully with the spicy carrot cake, but if you'd prefer, you can simply top the cake with whipped cream.

1 cup sugar
2 large eggs
1/4 cup water
1/3 cup sunflower oil
1 1/2 cups all-purpose flour
1 tsp. vanilla extract
1 tsp. baking powder
1/2 tsp. baking soda

1 tsp. ground cinnamon
1 tsp. ground ginger
1 cup peeled and finely shredded carrots
for the frosting
1 1/2 cups confectioners' sugar, sifted
1 1/2–2 tbsp. orange juice
1/4 cup chopped walnuts

In a large bowl with a mixer, cream together the sugar, eggs, water, and oil. Lightly mix in the flour, vanilla, baking powder, baking soda, and cinnamon, and ginger until just blended. Using a metal spoon, stir in the shredded carrots. Grease the inside of the slow cooker pot with butter or spray with oil. Pour in the batter, and spread it out evenly. Place a thickness of 4 or 5 paper towels across the top of the slow cooker, and place the lid on top. Cook on low for just over 2 hours, or until a toothpick inserted in the center comes out clean. Remove the pot from the slow cooker, and let the cake cool for 20 minutes. Then run a knife around the edge of the cake and turn it out onto a wire rack. Let cool completely. In a small bowl, mix the sugar with enough orange juice to make it slightly runny. Spread it over the top of the cake, and sprinkle with the walnuts.

Makes 6–8 servings

chocolate caramel cheesecake

see variations page 250

Quite often cheesecake baked in the oven will crack as it cools, but cooked in the slow cooker, the steam makes the cheesecake silky smooth while helping to prevent cracking. So do not remove the cover until the end.

1 1/4 cups chocolate-covered graham
   cracker crumbs
1/4 cup chopped walnuts
2 tbsp. sugar
1/4 cup butter, melted
12 oz. cream cheese, softened
2/3 cup sugar

2 tbsp. flour
2 large eggs
1 tsp. vanilla extract
2/3 cup sour cream
1/2 cup semisweet chocolate chips
1/2 cup butterscotch chips

In a large bowl, combine the graham cracker crumbs, walnuts, 2 tablespoons sugar, and the butter. Pat into the bottom of a 7-inch springform pan and set aside. In a large bowl, beat the cream cheese until smooth and mix in 2/3 cup sugar. Add flour, eggs, and vanilla, and beat again. Stir in the sour cream, and pour into the springform pan. Melt the chocolate and butterscotch chips separately in small bowls in the microwave and drizzle each over the cheesecake, one at a time. Using a knife, swirl them into the cheesecake, marbling the mixture. Place a rack in the bottom of the slow cooker, and fold two 24-inch-long pieces of aluminum foil in half, then again, making two long strips. Place them over the rack, making a cross, in order to lift the pan out at the end of cooking time. Place the springform pan on the rack and foil, making sure it is level. Cover and cook on high for 2 1/2–3 hours. Turn off the slow cooker, do not remove the lid, and leave for 1 hour. Remove the cheesecake from the slow cooker, and cool completely, before chilling in the refrigerator.
Makes 6 servings

chocolate walnut brownies

see variations page 251

These are very moist and chocolatey brownies. Putting the paper towels across the top of the slow cooker helps the brownies cook properly, by stopping moisture from dropping onto the surface of the cake and making it soggy.

1/2 cup vegetable oil
1 cup brown sugar
2 tbsp. butter
2 large eggs
1 cup water
1/4 cup chopped walnuts
1/4 cup semisweet chocolate chips
1/2 cup unsweetened cocoa powder

3/4 cup all-purpose flour
1 tbsp. cornstarch
1/4 tsp. baking powder
1/4 tsp. baking soda
1/4 tsp. salt
1 1/4 cups granulated sugar
vanilla ice cream, to serve

In a small saucepan, warm the oil, brown sugar, and butter until the sugar has melted. In a large bowl, lightly beat the eggs and stir in the water. In another bowl, mix the walnuts, chocolate chips, cocoa powder, flour, cornstarch, baking powder, baking soda, salt, and granulated sugar. Add to the eggs with the oil and butter and mix well. Pour batter into the slow cooker, place 2 layers of paper towels across the top of the slow cooker, and place the lid on top. Cook on low for 2 hours. Check with a toothpick after 1 3/4 hours. The toothpick should have a small amount of cake on it; the brownies should not be overcooked and should be slightly underdone in the middle. Serve warm with vanilla ice cream.

Makes 6 servings

peach cobbler

see variations page 252

The cinnamon and nutmeg in this cobbler give it a wonderful aroma as it cooks, and the taste is simply divine. Serve it with vanilla ice cream.

1/2 cup melted butter
1 cup flour
1 cup sugar
2 tsp. baking powder
pinch salt
2/3 cup whole milk, room temperature

1 large egg, room temperature
1 (28-oz.) can sliced peaches, drained
1/2 cup sugar
1 tsp. ground cinnamon
1/2 tsp. ground nutmeg
vanilla ice cream, to serve

Grease the slow cooker pot, and turn on the slow cooker to low. Pour in the melted butter. In a large bowl, mix together the flour, sugar, baking powder, and salt. Stir in the milk and egg, and pour mixture on top of the melted butter. In another bowl, mix the sliced peaches with the sugar and spices. Add to the batter in the slow cooker, and do not stir. Lay 2 or 3 layers of paper towels across the top of the slow cooker, place the cover on top, and cook on low for 4 hours. Serve warm or chilled.

Makes 6 servings

stuffed apples

see variations page 253

Baked, stuffed apples make excellent standby winter desserts. Served warm with whipped cream, they are easy, healthy, and delicious. Score around the center of each apple before cooking to prevent them from bursting.

6–8 medium apples
2 tsp. lemon juice
2–3 tbsp. raisins
1/4 cup granulated sugar
1 tsp. ground cinnamon

3/4 cup orange juice
1 tsp. grated orange rind
1/2 cup apple cider
1/2 cup brown sugar
whipped cream, to serve

Using a sharp knife, score a line around the center of each apple and remove the core with an apple corer. Brush the hollowed out core of each apple with a little lemon juice to prevent discoloration. In a small bowl, mix the raisins, sugar, and half the cinnamon. Fill each apple. Put the apples into the slow cooker, standing them upright, and add the orange juice, the rest of the cinnamon, orange rind, apple cider, and brown sugar to the slow cooker. Cover and cook on low for 3–4 hours. Serve warm with whipped cream.

Makes 6–8 servings

pears poached in red wine

see variations page 254

This dessert is best when served chilled, with a generous spoonful of lightly whipped cream on the side. You can prepare the pears two days ahead if you wish. Just keep them chilled in the refrigerator.

3/4 cup sugar
2/3 cup water
2/3 cup red wine
1 (1-inch) cinnamon stick

6 firm pears
2 tsp. cornstarch mixed with 3 tbsp. water
whipped cream, to serve

Place the sugar, water, wine, and cinnamon stick in a medium saucepan. Heat until the sugar has dissolved. Transfer to the slow cooker. Peel the pears, leaving on the stalks, and place them in the syrup in the slow cooker. Cover and cook on low for 2 hours, until the pears are transparent. With a slotted spoon, transfer the pears from the slow cooker to a serving plate. Mix the cornstarch with a little water and add to the syrup in the slow cooker, stirring well. Leaving the cover off, cook for 15 minutes or until the syrup has thickened. Let the syrup cool, then spoon it over the pears. Chill. Serve with lightly whipped cream.

Makes 6 servings

apple brown betty

see variations page 255

A mixture of breadcrumbs, butter, and apples, this is one of the oldest desserts in America, dating from colonial times. You can save it for a special treat.

6 cups apples, peeled, cored, and sliced 1/4 inch thick
2 tbsp. lemon juice
4 cups fresh breadcrumbs
2/3 cup unsalted butter, melted, plus extra for greasing
1 1/2 cups light brown sugar

2 tsp. ground cinnamon
1 tsp. ground ginger
1/2 tsp. ground allspice
1/2 tsp. ground nutmeg
2/3 cup raisins
vanilla ice cream, to serve

Put the apple slices into a large bowl, mix in the lemon juice, and turn the apples around to coat them with the juice to prevent discoloration.

In another bowl, mix the breadcrumbs and 2/3 cup butter together with the brown sugar, cinnamon, ginger, allspice, nutmeg, and raisins. Grease the bottom and sides of the slow cooker pot with butter. Make a layer of apples, then the breadcrumb mixture, then apples—making a total of 2 or 3 layers, finishing with the breadcrumbs. Place 2 layers of paper towels across the top of the slow cooker, place the lid on top, and cook on low for 3–4 hours, until the apples are tender. Serve with vanilla ice cream, and perhaps caramel sauce.

Makes 6 servings

rice pudding

see variations page 256

This childhood favorite is delicious hot or cold, plain or with maple syrup, chocolate sauce, or fruit of any kind.

5 1/4 cups whole milk
4 1/2 ounces Arborio rice (just under 3/4 cup)
1/2 cup sugar

Place all the ingredients in the slow cooker and stir to combine. Cover and cook on low for 6–8 hours.

Makes 6 servings

blueberry vanilla crème brûlée

see variations page 257

The best way of making the crisp caramel on top of a crème brûlée is with a blowtorch. If you do not own one, you can place the desserts under a very hot broiler to caramelize the sugar.

1/2 cup fresh or frozen blueberries
1 vanilla pod
2 1/2 cups heavy cream

4 large egg yolks
1/4 cup sugar
3 tablespoons sugar for topping

Divide the blueberries into 4 individual ramekins. Set aside. Slit the vanilla pod lengthwise and put it and the cream in the top of a double boiler or in a heatproof bowl over a pan of hot water. Bring to just below the boiling point, remove from the heat, and leave for 15 minutes to infuse the flavors. Lift the vanilla pod out of the cream, and scrape the black seeds out of the pod and back into the cream. In a medium pitcher, whisk the egg yolks with 1/4 cup sugar. Whisk the cream into the eggs, carefully pour the egg-cream mixture into the dishes on top of the blueberries, and place the ramekins in the bottom of the slow cooker. Add enough water to come halfway up the sides of the dishes, being very careful not to splash water into the ramekins. Cover and cook on low for 3–3 1/2 hours, until the desserts are set. They should have a slight wobble in the center. Using oven gloves, lift the pot out of the slow cooker unit and let cool until you can lift the ramekins out of the pot. Refrigerate for several hours or overnight. Sprinkle the tops of the crème brûlées with the rest of the sugar and either use a blowtorch or place under a preheated broiler until the sugar turns to caramel. Chill again before serving.

Makes 4 servings

chocolate tapioca pudding

see variations page 258

One of the problems of cooking puddings on the stove is that the milk might burn on the bottom of the saucepan. When you switch to the slow cooker, that problem is completely eliminated.

8 cups milk
1 1/4 cups sugar
1 cup small pearl tapioca

3 large eggs
1 tsp. almond extract
1 tbsp. unsweetened cocoa powder

In the slow cooker, mix together the milk, sugar, and tapioca. Cover and cook on high for 2–3 hours, or until the tapioca has softened slightly. In a large bowl, whisk together the eggs, almond extract, and cocoa powder. To temper the milk (to prevent the eggs from scrambling), measure out 1/2 cup of hot milk and tapioca and stir it into the eggs. Do this twice more, then pour the mixture into the slow cooker and stir well. Cover and cook on high for another 30 minutes to an hour, or until the tapioca has begun to swell and thicken. Turn off the slow cooker, and remove the cover. Leave for another hour to thicken more, stir again, cook, and refrigerate to chill completely.

Makes 6 servings

white chocolate & cherry bread pudding

see variations page 259

They do say that if you are a real chocoholic, you will find white chocolate irresistible. This is a delicious way of using up leftover bread, and wonderful served with a cherry sauce or whipped cream.

1/2 cup dried cherries	4 large eggs
2 tbsp. bourbon or apple cider	1/2 cup sugar
2 tbsp. butter for greasing	1 1/2 cups half-and-half
6 cups cubed French bread	1 tsp. vanilla extract
4 oz. good-quality white chocolate, coarsely chopped	whipped cream, to serve

In a medium bowl, soak the cherries in the bourbon or cider for 1 hour, then drain and set aside. Generously butter the slow cooker pot, and place half the bread cubes in the bottom. Scatter half the cherries and half the chocolate on top of the bread, add the other half of the bread and top with the rest of the cherries and chocolate.

In a medium bowl, whisk the eggs and sugar together, then whisk in the half-and-half and vanilla extract. Carefully pour the mixture over the bread, cherries, and chocolate, gently pressing the bread down into the liquid. Cover and cook on high for 1 3/4 hours, without lifting the lid, until the pudding is puffed and set. The timing is quite critical. Serve warm with whipped cream.

Makes 6 servings

variations

sticky toffee pudding

see base recipe page 229

sticky toffee pudding with chocolate
Prepare the basic recipe, replacing 2 tablespoons flour with 2 tablespoons unsweetened cocoa powder, sifted.

sticky toffee pudding with apples & cinnamon
Prepare the basic recipe, omitting the sauce, and replacing the ground ginger with ground cinnamon. Add 1 peeled and diced apple to the mixture with the dates. Serve with whipped cream.

sticky toffee pudding with orange & rum
Prepare the basic recipe, adding 2 tablespoons rum, and the grated rind of 1 orange to the mixture with the dates. Add 2 tablespoons rum and 1/2 cup chopped dates to the sauce.

figgy pudding
Prepare the basic recipe, omitting the ground ginger. Add the grated rind of 1 orange and 1/2 cup chopped dried figs to the mixture with the dates.

carrot cake with orange frosting

see base recipe page 231

lemon drizzle cake
Prepare the basic recipe, omitting the frosting, water, and carrots. Increase
the oil to 1/2 cup and add the grated rind of 2 lemons to the batter. Prick
the warm cake and pour over lemon drizzle made by mixing the juice of
2 lemons with 1/2 cup sugar.

apple & pecan cake with chocolate frosting
Prepare the basic recipe, omitting the frosting, water, and carrots. Increase
the oil to 1/2 cup and add 1 1/2 cups peeled and finely chopped apples to
the batter. Make icing by heating 1 tablespoon unsweetened cocoa powder
with 3 tablespoons butter. Gently cook 1 minute, remove from heat, and mix
in 3 tablespoons evaporated milk and 1 cup confectioners' sugar. Spread
over cooled cake.

pear & chocolate cake with whipped cream
Prepare the basic recipe, omitting the water, carrots, and 2 tablespoons
flour. Increase the oil to 1/2 cup. Add 2 tablespoons sifted cocoa powder
and 1 1/2 cups peeled and chopped pears. Replace the frosting with
whipped cream.

chocolate caramel cheesecake

see base recipe page 232

chocolate peanut butter cheesecake
Prepare the basic recipe, replacing the butterscotch chips with peanut butter chips and the caramel fudge ice cream topping with chocolate fudge ice cream topping.

white chocolate cheesecake
Prepare the basic recipe, replacing the chocolate and butterscotch chips with 1 cup white chocolate chips.

chocolate chip cookie dough cheesecake
Prepare the basic recipe, omitting the chocolate and butterscotch chips. Take 1 cup of uncooked chocolate chip cookie dough and, using your clean and floured hands, roll into small balls. Drop them into the cheesecake, spacing them out evenly and pushing them down to cover them with the cheesecake mixture completely.

blueberry cheesecake
Prepare the basic recipe, omitting the chocolate and butterscotch chips. Scatter 1 cup fresh blueberries into the cheesecake, pushing them down to cover them with the cheesecake mixture completely.

chocolate walnut brownies

see base recipe page 235

rocky road brownies
Prepare the base recipe. Ten minutes before the end of the cooking time, scatter 1/2 cup mini-marshmallows onto the brownies.

double chocolate walnut brownies
Prepare the basic recipe, adding 1/4 cup white chocolate chips at the same time as the walnuts.

chocolate ginger brownies
Prepare the basic recipe, adding 1 tablespoon molasses to the oil and butter and 2 teaspoons ground ginger to the flour mix.

chocolate peanut butter brownies
Prepare the basic recipe, adding 3 tablespoons peanut butter to the eggs and water, and mixing well.

variations

peach cobbler

see base recipe page 236

cherry cobbler
Prepare the basic recipe, replacing the peaches with pitted, drained canned cherries.

apricot–almond cobbler
Prepare the basic recipe, replacing the peaches with canned apricots. Add 1 teaspoon almond extract to the batter and scatter a few toasted, sliced almonds on top of the cobbler when finished cooking.

peach–raspberry cobbler
Prepare the basic recipe, adding 1/2 cup raspberries with the peaches.

apple–blackberry cobbler
Prepare the basic recipe, omitting the peaches, cinnamon, and nutmeg, and substituting 1 drained (14-ounce) can apple slices and 1 drained (14-ounce) can blackberries.

variations

stuffed apples

see base recipe page 237

stuffed apples with blueberries & almonds
Prepare the basic recipe, omitting the raisins and the cinnamon in the filling. Substitute 3 tablespoons fresh or frozen blueberries and 2 teaspoons chopped almonds.

stuffed apples in sweet white wine
Prepare the basic recipe, omitting the orange juice, orange rind, and apple cider. Substitute 1 1/4 cups sweet white wine.

stuffed apples with dates & pecans
Prepare the basic recipe, omitting the raisins and the cinnamon in the filling. Substitute 3 tablespoons pitted and chopped dried dates and 1 tablespoon chopped pecans.

stuffed apples with apricots & almonds
Prepare the basic recipe, omitting the raisins and the cinnamon in the filling. Substitute 3 tablespoons chopped dried apricots and 1 tablespoon chopped almonds. Replace 1/4 cup apple cider with 1/4 cup Grand Marnier.

variations

pears poached in red wine

see base recipe page 238

peaches poached in marsala
Prepare the basic recipe, replacing the pears with peaches and the red wine
with marsala.

pears poached in red wine with brandy
Prepare the basic recipe, adding 2 tablespoons brandy to the wine
in the saucepan.

pears poached in vanilla & sweet white wine
Prepare the basic recipe, omitting the water, red wine, and cinnamon stick.
Substitute 2 split vanilla pods and 1 1/3 cups sweet white wine.

pears poached in port wine
Prepare the basic recipe, replacing the water and red wine with 1 1/3 cups
port wine.

variations

apple brown betty

see base recipe page 241

apple–rhubarb brown betty
Prepare the basic recipe, replacing 1/2 cup apples with 1/2 cup
chopped rhubarb.

peach–cranberry brown betty
Prepare the basic recipe, replacing half the apples with pitted and sliced
peaches. Add 1/4 cup dried cranberries to the apples and peaches.

crunchy apricot brown betty
Prepare the basic recipe, replacing half the apples with pitted and sliced
apricots. Add 1/2 cup chopped walnuts to the breadcrumbs.

apple–pear brown betty with chocolate sauce
Prepare the basic recipe, replacing half the apples with peeled, cored, and sliced
pears. Serve with chocolate sauce.

variations

rice pudding

see base recipe page 242

rice pudding with coconut
Prepare the basic recipe, replacing 2 cups of milk with 2 cups of coconut milk. Best served chilled.

rice pudding with apricots & raspberry coulis
Prepare the basic recipe, and refrigerate until cold. Top each portion with half an apricot and drizzle with raspberry coulis. To make the coulis, rub 2 cups fresh raspberries through a sieve to remove the seeds, then beat in 4 tablespoons sifted confectioners' sugar a tablespoonful at a time.

rice pudding with raisins, cherries & almonds
Prepare the basic recipe. Ten minutes before the end of the cooking time, add 1/3 cup each of raisins, pitted fresh dark cherries, and sliced almonds.

spicy rice pudding with cashews & cardamom
Prepare the basic recipe, adding 1/4 cup unsalted roasted cashews and 1/2 teaspoon cardamom seeds 10 minutes before the end of the cooking time.

blueberry vanilla crème brûlée

see base recipe page 245

cherry vanilla crème brûlée
Prepare the basic recipe, replacing the blueberries with pitted cherries.

lemon crème brulee
Prepare the basic recipe, omitting the blueberries. Add the grated rind of
1 lemon to the egg yolks with the sugar.

chocolate crème brûlée
Prepare the basic recipe, omitting the blueberries, and adding 1/2 cup
melted semisweet chocolate chips to the cream after bringing it to just
under boiling point.

maple crème brûlée
Prepare the basic recipe, omitting the blueberries. Add 1/4 cup pure maple
syrup to the eggs while whisking.

coconut crème brûlée
Prepare the basic recipe, omitting 1 cup heavy cream and the blueberries.
Substitute 1 cup coconut milk and add 1/4 cup flaked sweetened coconut.

variations

chocolate tapioca pudding

see base recipe page 246

chocolate & cherry tapioca pudding
Prepare the basic recipe, adding 1/2 cup dried cherries to the slow cooker about 30–60 minutes before the end of the cooking time.

chocolate & pear tapioca pudding
Prepare the basic recipe. Add a few slices of fresh peeled, cored, and sliced pear to each serving.

vanilla tapioca pudding
Prepare the basic recipe, replacing the almond extract and the cocoa powder with 1 teaspoon vanilla extract. Serve with fresh strawberries and raspberries and a generous dollop of whipped cream.

chocolate & cinnamon tapioca pudding
Prepare the basic recipe, replacing the almond extract with 1/2 teaspoon ground cinnamon. Serve with cooled stewed apples.

white chocolate & cherry bread pudding

see base recipe page 247

dark chocolate & cranberry bread pudding
Prepare the basic recipe, replacing the white chocolate with dark chocolate.
Replace the cherries with dried cranberries.

white chocolate & blueberry bread pudding
Prepare the basic recipe, replacing the cherries with dried blueberries.

white chocolate, pineapple & coconut bread pudding
Prepare the basic recipe, omitting the cherries. Add 3 tablespoons chopped
glacé pineapple and 1/2 cup flaked sweetened coconut to the layers.

white chocolate & cherry bread pudding with cherry sauce
Prepare the basic recipe. Make cherry sauce by heating the juice from
1 (16-ounce) can pitted red cherries with 1 tablespoon each of cornstarch,
sugar, and lemon juice. Simmer for 2 minutes, remove from heat, and add
the cherries. Serve warm with the bread pudding, and also with whipped
cream, if desired.

preserves, stocks & drinks

Weekends are a great time to use your slow

cooker for something other than meals or

desserts. From preserving a glut of available fruit,

preparing a delicious stock for the following week,

or making an alcoholic punch for a party, your

slow cooker is invaluable.

summer fruit compote

see variations page 274

A compote is fruit cooked in syrup for roughly an hour or two. Serve it hot or cold, for dessert or on cereal, or with yogurt at breakfast.

3 cups strawberries
3 cups raspberries
3 cups plums, pitted
3 cups cherries, pitted

3 cups blueberries
3 cups blackberries
1 cup sugar

Wash and drain the fruit. Cut the strawberries and plums into pieces the same size as the raspberries. Place all the fruit and the sugar in the slow cooker, cover, and cook on low for 2–3 hours.

Makes 6 servings

lemon curd

see variations page 275

This curd is so versatile, you can make little lemon tarts, a meringue pie, or serve it on scones or over ice cream for dessert.

grated rind and juice from 8 lemons
1 1/2 cups sugar
3/4 cup unsalted butter, diced

3 large eggs
2 large egg yolks

In a medium saucepan, over low heat, heat the lemon juice, lemon rind, sugar, and butter together until the sugar has dissolved and the butter has melted, stirring occasionally. In a medium bowl, beat the eggs and egg yolks together and strain them into the lemon juice, mixing until blended. Pour into a 1-quart baking dish that will fit into your slow cooker, and cover with aluminum foil. Tie on foil with string, making a handle to easily lift the bowl, and place into the slow cooker. Pour in hot water to come halfway up the side of the dish, cover, and cook on low for 2–3 hours. Stir once or twice during cooking, if possible. Sterilize 5 half-pint jars, pour in the curd, and seal. Cover, label, and refrigerate for up to 4 weeks.

Makes approximately 5 jars

cranberry sauce

see variations page 276

This is the easiest cranberry sauce you will ever make! The stovetop method is definitely out of fashion.

8 cups fresh cranberries
2 cups sugar
1 cup freshly squeezed orange juice

Pick over the cranberries and remove any stems. Place them in the slow cooker with the sugar and orange juice. Cover and cook on high for 2–2 1/2 hours. At the end of the cooking time, the cranberries will have popped open. Turn the heat off, remove the cover, and let cool to room temperature. Store in the refrigerator for up to 3 weeks.

Makes 6 cups

apple butter

see variations page 277

There is no butter in this dish. Its name is because of its thick creamy texture and because it is often used as a spread on bread. Apple butter is a concentrated form of applesauce and lasts much longer.

2/3 cup granulated sugar
2/3 cup brown sugar
1 tsp. ground cinnamon
1/2 tsp. freshly ground nutmeg

1/2 tsp. ground gingerroot
1/4 tsp. ground cloves
1/4 tsp. salt
15–16 apples, peeled, cored, and finely chopped

In a medium bowl, mix the sugars with the spices and salt. Place all the apples in the slow cooker, and sprinkle with the sugar and spice mixture. Stir it all together, cover, and cook on low for 12 hours, until the mixture has thickened and turned dark brown as the sugar caramelizes. If you like a smoother texture, stir with a whisk. Pour into sterilized jars and store for a month in the refrigerator, or freeze.

Makes 5 jars

preserved plums

see variations page 278

With this dish, you can halve the plums and remove the pits, or leave them whole, with the pits inside. If you like a more mushy texture, cut the plums into quarters before cooking.

3 lbs. ripe plums (about 12–14), washed
2 cups granulated sugar
1 tsp. ground cinnamon
1/2 tsp. ground ginger

1/4 cup water
2 tbsp. cornstarch

Place the plums—halved or whole—in the slow cooker with the sugar and spices. In a small bowl, mix the cornstarch with the water and add to the plums. Cover and cook on low for 3–4 hours. Pour into sterilized jars and store in the refrigerator for 2 weeks, or freeze.

Makes 3 jars

ultimate tomato sauce

see variations page 279

This is the ultimate tomato sauce to serve over pasta. The long slow cooking ensures a rich flavor that is missing from most stovetop sauces. It is a great staple to keep in the refrigerator, and it freezes well.

2 tbsp. extra-virgin olive oil
2 large onions, finely chopped
4 cloves garlic, crushed
3 tsp. dried basil
3 tsp. dried oregano
1 cup vegetable stock
1 vegetable stock cube (or chicken)
2 (14-oz.) cans chopped tomatoes in juice
2 (14-oz.) cans tomato puree

3 (6-oz.) cans tomato paste
2 celery stalks, trimmed and diced small
2 large carrots, peeled and diced small
1 tbsp. soy sauce
1 tbsp. Worcestershire sauce
1 tbsp. sugar
salt and freshly ground black pepper, to taste
1/2 cup freshly chopped basil leaves

In a large skillet, heat the oil and cook the onions and garlic for 5 minutes, or until softened. Add the herbs and cook for 1 minute. Transfer to the slow cooker and add the rest of the ingredients except the fresh basil. Cover and cook on low for 6-8 hours. One hour before the end of the cooking time, check that the sauce is not too thick. If it is, thin with a little water or vegetable stock. Taste, and adjust the seasoning if necessary. Stir in 1/2 cup freshly chopped basil leaves, and finish cooking.

Makes approximately 10 cups

beef stock

see variations page 280

This recipe produced a rich meaty broth. Ask your butcher for oxtail, shanks, or any meaty beef bones. Store or freeze it in usable portions.

1 1/2 lbs. beef bones
1/2 lb. stewing steak, diced
1 large onion, quartered
1 large carrot, peeled and halved
1 celery stalk, cut into thirds
2 tbsp. vegetable oil
2 cloves garlic, chopped

1 tsp. black peppercorns
4 cloves
1 tsp. dried thyme
1 tsp. dried rosemary
1 tsp. dried parsley
2 bay leaves

Heat the oven to 425°F. Place the bones, beef, and vegetables in a large roasting pan, drizzle with the oil, and turn the bones to coat all over. Sprinkle with the garlic and herbs, and roast in the oven for about an hour. Turn over the bones and vegetables after about a half hour. Remove from the oven and transfer the bones, beef, and vegetables to the slow cooker. Cover with water (about 6 cups) and cook on low for 10–12 hours. Pour the stock through a sieve, cover, and refrigerate. Discard the bones and vegetables. When the stock has thoroughly chilled, remove the fat from the surface. Store in the refrigerator for 4–5 days, or freeze for up to 6 months.

Makes about 6 cups

mulled red wine

see variations page 281

Mulled red wine is great to serve at a party, especially one in the winter. When the wine is ready, leave it in the slow cooker so it will stay warm for your guests as they come in from the cold. There is no point in splashing out on great wine and brandy, as the sugar and spices will alter its flavor, opt for cheaper brands and save yourself the difference!

2 bottles red wine
1/2 cup brandy
1 cup light brown sugar

1 orange
8 cloves
1 cinnamon stick, broken into 3 pieces

Pour the wine and brandy into the slow cooker, add the sugar and stir. Cut the orange into 8 segments and stud each segment with a clove. Add to the slow cooker with the cinnamon stick. Cook on low for 3–4 hours. Serve in heatproof glasses.

Makes 8–10 glasses

variations

summer fruit compote

see base recipe page 261

summer pudding
Prepare the compote and let cool. Line a 1-quart baking dish with thin crustless slices white bread. Spoon the compote into the dish and place slices of bread on the top. Cover with plastic wrap and chill for 24 hours before serving.

peach fruit compote
Instead of the basic recipe, prepare the compote with 8 pitted and sliced large fresh peaches. Add 1 cup brown sugar, 1/2 cup brandy, 1 teaspoon vanilla extract, and 1 teaspoon ground ginger. Add 4 tablespoons butter, cover, and cook on low for 2 hours.

summer fruit compote with shortbread
Prepare the compote. For shortbread, sift 1 cup flour, pinch salt, 1/4 cup fine cornmeal, 1/3 cup sugar into a large bowl. Rub in 1 stick butter. Press into a 7-inch tart pan and chill for 30 minutes. Prick with a fork, mark into triangles, bake for 40–45 minutes at 325°F, until golden brown. Serve on the side.

lemon curd

see base recipe page 263

lemon & lime curd
Prepare the basic recipe, replacing 2 lemons with 3 limes.

orange & lemon curd
Prepare the basic recipe, replacing 2 lemons with 2 oranges.

baby lemon meringue pies
Prepare the basic recipe. Fill 12 individual partly baked pastry crusts with a little lemon curd and top with meringue, made by whisking 2 egg whites with 1/2 cup superfine sugar until very stiff. Divide between the pies and bake at 275°F for about 20 minutes, or until the meringue is crisp and golden. Cool and serve warm.

raspberry curd
Prepare the basic recipe, omitting 4 lemons and substituting 2 cups raspberries, pushed through a sieve to remove the seeds. Only use the rind from 1 lemon.

lemon & passion fruit curd
Prepare the basic recipe, omitting 2 lemons and substituting 1/2 cup passion fruit pulp, scooped out from about 5 passion fruits.

variations

cranberry sauce

see base recipe page 264

cranberry & blueberry sauce
Prepare the basic recipe, adding 2 cups fresh blueberries and an extra
2 cups sugar to the slow cooker with the cranberries.

cranberry sauce with orange marmalade
Prepare the basic recipe, adding 1/2 cup orange marmalade to the
slow cooker.

cranberry sauce with cinnamon & nutmeg
Prepare the basic recipe, adding 2 teaspoons ground cinnamon and
2 teaspoons ground nutmeg.

cranberry relish
Prepare the basic recipe, adding 1 peeled, cored, and chopped pear and
1/4 cup chopped dried dates.

cranberry & apple sauce
Prepare the basic recipe, adding 2 peeled, cored and chopped apples.

variations

apple butter

see base recipe page 267

apple & cranberry butter
Prepare the basic recipe, omitting 3–4 apples and substituting 3 cups
fresh cranberries.

apple & apricot butter
Prepare the basic recipe, omitting 3–4 apples and substituting 3 cups fresh
apricots, pitted and finely chopped. No need to peel.

apple butter tortillas
Prepare the basic recipe. Warm 4 flour tortillas, one at a time, in a little oil in a
skillet. Then spread each one with apple butter and roll up. Sprinkle with a little
cinnamon sugar. Place back in the skillet to caramelize the sugar, and serve
hot. Delicious served with vanilla ice cream and butterscotch sauce.

apple & cherry butter
Prepare the basic recipe, omitting 3–4 apples and substituting 3 cups pitted
fresh cherries.

variations

preserved plums

see base recipe page 268

preserved peaches
Prepare the basic recipe, replacing the plums with peaches. Remove seeds.
No need to remove skins.

preserved cherries
Prepare the basic recipe, replacing the plums with 3 pounds cherries, with or
without pits.

preserved figs
Prepare the basic recipe, replacing the plums with figs, washed and peeled.
Omit the cornstarch and water, and substitute the juice of 2 lemons.

hot fruit salad
Prepare the basic recipe, replacing 2 pounds plums with 1 pound peeled,
cored, and chopped pears and I pound peeled, cored, and chopped apples.
Serve hot from the pot, with cold ice cream.

preserved apples & blackberries
Prepare the basic recipe, replacing the plums with 2 pounds peeled, cored,
and chopped apples and 1 pound blackberries.

variations

ultimate tomato sauce

see base recipe page 269

spicy tomato sauce with artichokes & sun-dried tomatoes
Prepare the basic recipe. When serving over pasta, add 1 canned artichoke
heart, broken into 3 pieces; 1 halved sun-dried tomato; and 1 finely chopped
mild green chili to each portion.

tomato & pepper sauce
Prepare the basic recipe, adding 4 roasted red bell peppers. Halve each pepper,
remove seeds, brush with a little vegetable oil, and broil until slightly
blackened. Cool slightly, slice, and add to the slow cooker with the rest of
the vegetables.

tomato sauce with meatballs
Prepare the basic recipe. Serve with meatballs. In a bowl, mix 1 pound ground
beef, 1 diced small onion, salt, and freshly ground black pepper. Using your
hands, form small to medium meatballs, roll in flour, and fry in very hot oil
until dark brown and partly cooked. Drain on paper towels for a few minutes.
Put in a baking dish with 3–4 cups tomato sauce, cover, and cook at 350°F
for 30 minutes. Serve with pasta.

variations

beef stock

see base recipe page 270

chicken stock
Prepare the basic recipe, omitting the bones and beef, and substituting a whole chicken, cut into pieces. Also add 1 teaspoon dried sage.

fish stock
Prepare the basic recipe, omitting the bones and beef. Put the fish and fish bones straight into the slow cooker with the vegetables. Omit the herbs, and substitute 2 teaspoons dried dillweed.

vegetable stock
Prepare the basic recipe, omitting the bones and beef and the oven-roasting. Add another carrot, 3 celery stalks, 2 washed and sliced leeks, and 1 tomato to the other vegetables in the slow cooker.

lamb stock
Prepare the basic recipe, omitting the bones and beef. Substitute 2 pounds lamb shanks.

veal stock
Prepare the basic recipe, replacing the bones and beef with the same quantity of veal bones and veal.

variations

mulled red wine

see base recipe page 273

mulled red wine with grand marnier
Prepare the basic recipe, adding 4 tablespoons Grand Marnier or Cointreau to the slow cooker with the wine.

mulled non-alcoholic punch
Prepare the basic recipe, omitting the red wine and brandy. Substitute 10 cups apple cider and 2 cups cranberry juice.

hot buttered cider
Prepare the basic recipe, omitting the red wine and brandy. Substitute 10 cups apple cider and 1 1/4 cups maple syrup. To serve, pour into heatproof glasses and top with a spoonful of spiced butter, made by mixing 1 cup softened butter with 1/2 cup brown sugar and 1 teaspoon each of nutmeg, allspice, and ginger.

mulled red wine with cherry brandy
Prepare the basic recipe, adding 4 tablespoons cherry brandy.

index